BREAST CANCER IN THE RAW

A Journey Through Generations

Verena Masencamp

United Kingdom

For more information, email verenamasencamp12@gmail.com

ISBN: 978-1-0369-2856-8

This book is dedicated to my father, Justus Fehrmann, who died 16 September 1985 from tongue cancer. He was my hero. I loved him deeply.

"Never be ashamed of a scar. It simply means you were stronger than whatever tried to hurt you."

—Philip Cochrane

Ernest Hemingway once said: “In our darkest moments, we don’t need advice.”

We don’t need solutions wrapped in pretty words.

We don’t need someone telling us to “stay positive” or “look on the bright side.”

We don’t need a road map out of the storm.

What we need is . . .

someone willing to sit in the dark with us,

someone who doesn’t flinch at our pain,

someone who understands that silence can be greater comfort than all the well-meaning words in the world.

Because when the weight is crushing, when the night feels endless—

We don’t need to be fixed.

We just need to know we’re not alone.

Contents

Introduction

My Precious Father—My First Encounter with Cancer

The room was bathed in soft golden light that filtered through the thin curtains, casting gentle shadows on the walls. Outside, the day was mild and crisp, typical of a spring morning in Cape Town, South Africa, where the earth still held the lingering warmth of the previous summer and the air was scented with the promise of new beginnings. The window was cracked open just enough to let in the whisper of a breeze, carrying with it the distant sounds of birdsong and the faint murmur of life continuing outside.

Inside, the room was quiet, save for the slow, rhythmic sound of my father's breathing, deep and steady, like the peaceful rhythm of a world at rest.

His body had grown frail over the past months, but his face—though pale and tired—held an expression of rare serenity. It was as though he had already made his peace, not with the idea of dying, but with the certainty that it was time to let go.

We sat beside him, watching him in the stillness. The only movement was the subtle rise and fall of his chest. Then in the quiet, he spoke—his voice a whisper, soft yet clear.

"There's a light . . . in the corner," he said, his eyes flickering towards the ceiling, where the light from the window seemed to meet the edge of the cupboard. His gaze lingered on the spot as if seeing something more than we could.

He paused, then looked at his dear wife, his tired eyes searching for her.

"I want to go home."

His words hung in the air, as simple as they were profound. There was no fear, no sadness—only the quiet acceptance of a man who knew his journey was nearly over. It was as though he had caught a glimpse of something beyond, something calling him home.

That morning with my father marked the first time I utterly understood the fragility of life. I had never encountered cancer before—never truly grasped its weight or the profound stillness it brings. But in that room, with the light from the window casting long shadows, I saw what peace could look like in the face of something so inevitable. His acceptance, his calm, the quiet strength with which he met the end—it all felt like a final gift to me.

I didn't know then that 38 years later, I would hear the same dreaded words: "Sorry to have to tell you, but you have cancer." Those words—so heavy, so cold—brought everything rushing back. In that instant, I was transported to that room, to the stillness of that spring morning, and I could almost hear my father's voice again—soft and certain—telling us, "I want to go home."

But this time, it was my turn to face it.

The peace that I once witnessed in him felt so distant now. The shock, the fear, the uncertainty—everything about the diagnosis felt like an entirely different weight. Yet somehow, his calmness—his quiet acceptance—lingered in the back of my mind, whispering, reminding me that there was a way through it, even if I didn't know how.

Looking back, I realise how much my father's nine-year struggle with cancer shaped the person he became—and shaped the way I would eventually face my own diagnosis.

It began in 1974 with a small spot on his tongue, something so simple, so unassuming. In South Africa in the early 1970s, the word *cancer* wasn't as familiar, and the treatments available were far less advanced than they are now. I remember how he would read aloud from the Bible every morning, his voice steady and familiar as he shared passages with my mother. But then he noticed a discomfort—a new awareness on his tongue, something that made speaking or reading more difficult. It worried him, so he went to see the general practitioner.

The doctor referred him to a plastic surgeon, who removed the spot and sent it away for a routine biopsy. We prayed that it had been enough—that it was just a small, benign thing. But the tests came back positive. It was cancer. And so began the long, painful journey. Two more operations followed over the next eight years, each one taking a little more of his tongue, a little more of his voice. Yet through it all, my father remained the same quiet, steady man. He never complained. Even when he had to change the way he ate or spoke, he did so with grace.

Then came the heart attack—the moment everything shifted. He ended up in Groote Schuur Hospital, the same hospital that had made history with the world's first heart transplant. It was there, in the ICU, that his medical records were shared and the doctors discovered the full extent of his cancer. They offered radiation treatment, and while he recovered from the heart attack, the plan was set in motion.

I still remember the day he went in for the radiation. The hospital had imported four radiation-active needles from overseas, and they were inserted through his jaw and mouth, then into his tongue. The room was small, sealed off, and we could see him only through a tiny window. He lay there for seven days and nights with those needles in place. It's impossible to fathom the pain, the horror, the isolation he must have felt. But I never heard him complain. When he came out of that room, weaker and exhausted, I remember thinking that no one could possibly endure what he had been through and still emerge with the same quiet strength.

The treatment had given him seven years of peace, a precious gift of time that we all hoped would stretch on forever. In that span, my father embraced life in a way that only someone who had faced death could. He travelled, laughed, shared memories, and made the most of every day. I often think back to that time with gratitude, knowing it was a gift we didn't realise would be so fleeting.

In 1984, my father, who was born in Switzerland, made plans to return to his homeland. It was something he had always wanted to do—to show my mom where he had been born and where he had grown up, then walk through the childhood memories that had shaped him. The trip was to be more than just a vacation; it was his way of reconnecting with his roots, with a part of himself that had been left behind in the years of living abroad.

But just before they were set to leave, my father noticed something—a familiar, unsettling sensation on his tongue. He knew what it meant. The cancer was back. Yet even with that knowledge, he was determined to go to Switzerland. Perhaps he knew it would be his last chance to visit, to walk those old streets, to feel the earth beneath his feet and breathe the air of his homeland one more time. And so he pushed through the fear, the pain, and the uncertainty, and they went.

My parents had a wonderful time there, taking in the beauty of the Swiss Alps, exploring the villages, and reconnecting with his roots. When they returned to Cape Town, there was a quiet joy in their faces and fulfilment in the way they shared stories from the trip. But underneath that joy, the cancer was already screaming for attention. It was as though it had been waiting for him to return, waiting for its turn to reclaim what it had lost.

Soon after, my father went into the hospital for another operation. His medical team sat down with him, and together, they made the difficult decision: They would remove his tongue entirely and attempt to rebuild a new one. The operation was scheduled for May 1985—a delicate, complex procedure that carried with it immense risks. But my father, as always, faced it with quiet determination, knowing that life had always demanded this kind of strength from him.

On my birthday, 12 May, my dad underwent a groundbreaking surgery at Tygerberg Hospital in Cape Town, South Africa. Doctors removed his entire tongue and reconstructed a new one using tissue from the inside of his arm, near his pulse—transplanting the nerves and blood supply to create a living, functional tongue. To cover the wound on his arm, they grafted skin from his thigh. In total, he had well over a thousand stitches in his mouth.

During his recovery, he had a tracheotomy, as his swollen tongue obstructed his airway. I can't even begin to imagine the pain and discomfort he endured. When I arrived at the hospital one evening, he was in agony, clutching his lower abdomen. I soon realised his catheter was full and forcing urine back into his body. Another time, I found him in a state of sheer panic while nurses attempted to suction his tracheotomy. Not understanding the procedure, he fought them, terrified that he couldn't breathe. I immediately asked them to stop, then calmly explained the process to him. Once he understood, he stopped resisting, reassured that he would soon be able to breathe again.

Moments like these make me wonder for the first time if health care professionals fully grasp the impact of their actions. I know that my father's were overworked and stretched thin. But at their core, nurses are meant to provide care—ensuring that patients feel safe, comfortable, and informed about what is happening to them. Despite these challenges and my misgivings during my own treatment, I will always be grateful for the chemotherapy nurses who cared for me. But I will share my subjective experiences with you later.

When my father came home from the hospital, he was cancer-free—at least for the moment. He weighed barely more than 60 kg, but he carried hope in his heart. Just a few weeks later, on 22 June 1985, my younger sister got married, and despite everything, my dad found the strength to give a speech. It was difficult for him, but he did it. He looked quite dapper in his new suit, a necessity after so much weight loss. For the first time in my life, I saw him without his beard—he had always been "the man with the beard." Though his face was still swollen, he was, and always would be, my dad—brilliant, kind, loving, and strong. We all held on to hope.

But that hope was short-lived. At his checkup the following week, doctors discovered that the cancer had spread to all his lymph nodes. There was nothing more they could do. That day, 24 June, was one of the saddest of my life. Less than three months later, on 16 September, he was gone.

His only wish was to die at home, and we made sure he did. My mother, my sisters, and I cared for him around the clock. I administered his morphine injections and tried everything to get him to eat, but he only grew thinner. A week before he passed, he asked my mom to stop bringing him food unless he requested it. He was ready. The suffering had simply become too much.

I had asked the doctors how he would die. I needed to be prepared. They told me it would be one of three ways: He could bleed to death, choke to death, or slowly dehydrate and slip away. You can imagine what I wished and prayed for.

Thankfully, he died from dehydration. On a Monday, he just slowly went into a coma as the day progressed. When the cancer nurse arrived late that afternoon, she gave him his morphine injection. Forty minutes later, he breathed his last. It was so quiet that we in the room didn't at first realise he was gone. Peacefully, quietly, he just slipped away.

My father, the jeweller and watchmaker.

As I faced my own diagnosis nearly 40 years later, the memories of my father's struggle became a source of strength and determination. I knew the journey through cancer would not be an easy one, but it was a path I had to walk. The advances in medical technology and treatments gave me hope that my story would have a different ending. The love and support of my family and friends surrounded me, just as they did for my father. I cherished every moment, every smile, and every hug. I leaned on my support system and embraced the advances in medicine that offered a fighting chance. Breast cancer was a formidable foe, but it did not define me, just as my father's cancer did not define him. I knew I was more than my diagnosis. And like my father, I strived to face the challenge with courage and grace.

This book is written for all women with breast cancer around the world, as well as their caregivers. If you are a cancer patient, know that you are not alone. One in three women get breast cancer. It is not a death sentence. Medical technology is amazing, and interventions bring hope.

You will go through so many different emotions. Just let them flow through you and then over you—then let them go.

I think that the stages of emotions you go through when receiving a cancer diagnosis could be similar to what you feel when a loved one dies. I am not saying it is definitely the same, but there are similarities. At first, there is disbelief. "Really? Cancer? Why me?" Then there are fear and sadness, as you know that nothing will be the same again. Slowly, as the reality sinks in and you learn more and more about your diagnosis, you may experience panic. But as time goes on, the best emotion to experience is just plain acceptance, together with a fighting spirit. Acceptance brings inner peace. Acceptance reduces stress. That doesn't mean you stop fighting. Oh no! You fight—you take every available treatment the professionals offer you.

People tell you to be positive. They tell you about someone they know who has or had cancer and how they dealt with it. Some people avoid you. Some offer meaningless platitudes. Let me tell you—just listen and then forget it. If you have not gone through this, you have no idea what the person is dealing with. So for those friends attempting to be comforting—sometimes all the breast cancer person needs is a listening ear. Not a bucket full of advice. Sometimes, she just needs someone to *be* there.

I know that everyone's journey is different, simply because we are all different. But here is to hoping you find some comfort within these pages. To hoping you see the rawness of breast cancer but also see the new beginnings when all the treatments are over. To hoping that you find a new zest for life because you have realised that life is short. It brings a freedom to be yourself, to laugh as loud as you want, to eat that piece of cake, to wear that dress, and to travel to those destinations you have dreamed of.

Because there is life through and after breast cancer.

Breast cancer, like tongue cancer, is a relentless adversary. It strikes fear into the hearts of those diagnosed, as well as their loved ones. But it also brings out the resilience and bravery that lie within. My father's battle with cancer taught me that, even in the face of the most daunting challenges, there is room for hope, for love, and for making the most of the time we have.

For me, the path ahead was uncertain, but one thing was clear: I was not alone. My father's spirit was with me, guiding me and giving me the strength to move forward. And just as he found joy and purpose in his cancer-free years, I vowed to do the same. This book, my life, and my dreams aren't just about battling cancer. They are about honouring his legacy and testifying to the enduring power of love and resilience.

Chapter 1 – The Diagnosis

11 September–24 September 2023
My Journey Begins

One night in September 2023, I was lying in bed, casually watching something on Netflix, when my right hand instinctively moved to my left breast. I don't know why—maybe I felt a twinge, or maybe it was just chance. But as I touched my breast, I discovered a tiny lump. It moved when I pressed it.

I remembered my mammogram from 2021, where I had been told I had harmless cysts, so I assumed this was probably the same. But something about it unsettled me. Every evening, I found myself checking the lump, unable to shake the nagging worry.

I talked to the lump in the middle of the night. "What are you? Are you a harmless alien invading my body? Or are you an enemy alien eating away at my body? You are so small; you can't possibly be a baddy."

I had to see my GP to settle my muddled mind. So I made an appointment for 25 September.

25 September 2023
First GP Appointment

While I was waiting to see the doctor, all kinds of thoughts kept going through my head. *Is it a cyst? Is it perhaps cancer?* I kept thinking it was definitely just a cyst, and I suppressed all other thoughts. The doctor examined me, and she, too, believed it was likely just a cyst. But she referred me to the breast clinic in Maidstone, England, to be sure.

That meant nine days of waiting to see the doctor at the breast clinic—days filled with emotions and thoughts that flooded my mind without being invited in. But the more I tried to lock the door on the different thoughts, the more they knocked with persistence to be let in.

As much as nine days feel like an eternity, I am also surprised at how quickly I got an appointment with the breast clinic.

5 October 2023
Breast Clinic Appointment

My appointment was at 10:45 at the Peggy Wood Clinic. Peggy Wood started a charity fund to relieve the sickness of patients suffering from leukaemia and cancer at Maidstone General Hospital in the County of Kent. Her foundation helps the hospital purchase equipment for the clinic.

I met with a breast cancer oncologist. She examined me and initially thought the lump seemed harmless—just another cyst. But then she felt under my arm. I was immediately aware of her concern. I could feel it in her body language.

She sent me off to have a mammogram. I was asked to wait. Then I was called back for a second mammogram—and asked to wait again. At best, a mammogram isn't the nicest experience. Having your breasts squashed between two metal plates is pretty painful and uncomfortable. To have to have two was really awful—especially because the need for a second one increased my worry tenfold.

Then I was called again and taken to another room, where a doctor performed an ultrasound on my breast and under my arm. He, too, found something under my arm that concerned him. So he decided to do a biopsy.

The nurse was lovely as she prepared me for the procedure. A thin needle was inserted into the lump, a piece of it was taken out, and a marker was left where he took the biopsy. I was lying on this hard bed, naked from my waist up, with my arms above my head, feeling exposed and scared and worried; however, none of these rampant emotions showed on my face. I am pretty good at keeping a calm exterior.

After the biopsy, I was asked to wait again. And then another mammogram (yes, another one!) to check that the marker was in place. Nearly three hours later, I was finally done and went straight to work, attempting to think nothing of it—or, at best, not think about it. Easier said than done!

I want to say that at no point did I really believe it could be cancer; however, there was a niggle. I was trying to convince myself it was just another cyst. So I did my level best to carry on with life—kind of unaware that I was about to cross the invisible line between BC (before cancer) and AC (after cancer).

24 October 2023
Dreaded Text Message

I received a text message, which I still have on my phone. It reads:

> Dear Anna Verena Masencamp, this is a reminder of your appointment with our BREAST CARE team at MAIDSTONE HOSPITAL on 26/10/2023 at 2.00pm. This will be a FACE-TO-FACE Appointment. To rearrange, reply REBOOK. If this appointment is no longer needed, reply CANCEL.

My landlady—who had also found a lump, had a mammogram, and undergone a biopsy at the same time I did and at the same clinic—received a text saying she was all clear and no further appointments were needed. That caused the small seed of worry in the back of my mind to niggle again. But still, I was attempting to convince myself that everything would be fine.

I arrived at the clinic early. The doctor was running late, and the nurse came out a few times to apologize. I wasn't too anxious—I was fortunately absorbed in my book. After a while, I did start to feel edgy. Eventually, I was called in.

I sat down across from the oncologist, and a nurse was seated nearby. The doctor glanced at her notes, then looked up at me and said the words that would change everything:

"I'm sorry to have to tell you, but you have cancer."

At that moment, you could have knocked me over with a feather. For a few seconds, I was completely stunned, just staring at her and the nurse. I have no idea what my facial expression said. I think I asked her if she was sure. She started talking about surgery, chemotherapy, medication, radiation—and this was where I zoned out.

Normally, in any moment of crisis, I become dead calm and practical. And for a short while, that is what I attempted to do. But I couldn't. I was just dumbstruck.

Fortunately, the specialist breast nurse was there during my appointment. After the oncologist delivered the news, the nurse gently guided me to another room—a space where I could breathe again. Then she handed me a cancer pack. Yes, that's a real thing: a folder filled with pamphlets, leaflets, information on support groups, treatment options, and everything else I was apparently supposed to process. I knew it might be useful later, but at that moment, it was just too overwhelming.

In that small consulting room, I became hyper-aware of the strangest details—the skilfully placed box of tissues on the table, the stacks of pamphlets about breast cancer and various medications. I found myself wondering, *Should I be crying?*

The nurse asked if I had any questions. My mind was blank—I couldn't think of a single question. She handed me a direct number to the nurses' station, reassuring me that I could call anytime if I had concerns or needed support. Then, in a small but thoughtful gesture, she led me out through a side door so I wouldn't have to walk through reception.

I appreciated that.

As I stepped outside, emotions crashed over me—disbelief, fear, worry, and an overwhelming need to speak to the people I love. I couldn't carry this alone. I had to share it.

I walked out of the doctors' rooms in a complete daze. I had barely stepped through the door when I felt my legs threaten to give way beneath me. But I knew I couldn't collapse—not here, not in the middle of the hospital corridor.

Somehow, I managed to call my sister Erika. The moment she answered, I felt a slight release from the crushing tension inside me. I can't remember what I said or what she said—only that I needed to hear her voice.

Still on autopilot, I made my way to the coffee shop and called my daughter and my son. I needed them to hear it directly from me. Again, I don't recall my exact words—only that I reassured them that I was fine and told them not to worry. But inside, I was deeply concerned about how they would process this news.

My son Richard lives in the United States. My daughter Samantha and my sister Erika both live in South Africa. They are all so far away, yet we are incredibly close. That distance suddenly felt unbearable.

And then, as if it were just another ordinary day, I went straight to work and did my night shift as a carer.

At the time, I was caring for an elderly man who was in his home and nearing the end of his life. There is something deeply special about spending the night with someone who struggles to sleep and feels anxious in the quiet hours while knowing I can bring him comfort. Holding his hand in the dead of night and sharing a cup of tea at two a.m. while he told me stories from his past were the best therapy for me—and I believe for him too—that I could have asked for.

As I stroked his arm, speaking softly to reassure him, I watched as he slowly drifted off to sleep. In those moments, I knew I had added a little bit of warmth to someone else's life. I am so privileged to do this work.

Meanwhile, the oncologist wasted no time. She scheduled an MRI for 13 November and a CT scan for 31 October. They needed to determine the stage of the cancer and how far it had spread before deciding on a treatment plan. Somewhere in all these conversations, I registered that the biopsy from my lymph node had confirmed cancer. But now they had to find the primary cancer—which should be in the breast. The MRI and CT scan would help them locate it. The mammogram had not picked up the cancer in the breast.

A Little Bit About Me

At the time of my diagnosis, I had been living in England for three years and worked as a carer. From a young age, I'd wanted to be a nurse. But life happened, and I didn't get the chance. So now, caring for the vulnerable and elderly was at least a part of my dream come true. At age 60, I was experiencing something of a personal renaissance. I had freed myself from an unhappy 27-year marriage and navigated an emotional divorce. I had acquired a postgraduate diploma in financial planning. Then I had moved to England and found my career as a professional carer, which provided me with an unprecedented level of financial stability and a life-giving calling. I worked in this role for three years—until the cancer diagnosis changed everything.

Chapter 2 – Waiting

25 October–30 October 2023
Tests and Waiting

I was still trying to come to grips with the reality of my diagnosis. The fact that inside me, an alien thing had taken root, something that didn't belong—something that was eating away at me and could ultimately take my life—caused anxiety.

In the stillness of the night, these thoughts grew into demons far bigger than I could have imagined. The uncertainty, the fear, the endless what-ifs—they all echoed louder in the dark.

I turned to Google, desperately searching for answers. I borrowed books from the library, trying to arm myself with knowledge. I started reading memoirs of those who had walked this road before me, searching for guidance, for hope. Their words became my lifeline, their strength my own.

I held on to positivity as best I could, even while the whispers of doubt screamed in my ear. I was reminded of my father's battle with cancer. I remembered how he calmly faced each challenge. Or at least he seemed calm—I don't really know how he felt deep down. I do know his faith was very strong.

One of the books I read was about a hospice nurse who was diagnosed with breast cancer. When she sat in the doctor's office as he told her she had breast cancer, she burst into tears, completely overwhelmed by emotion. She struggled to regain control, drowning in the weight of it all.

Eleven days had passed since I'd heard those life-altering words: "You have breast cancer." In those 11 days, I felt more emotions than I even knew existed. Yet I hadn't shed a single tear. It struck me how differently we all react—how no two cancer journeys are the same, simply because no two people are the same.

31 October 2023
CT Scan Day

The day arrived for the CT (computed tomography) scan—basically a diagnostic imaging procedure that uses a combination of X-rays and computer technology to produce images of the inside of my body.

They did the CT scan in buildings that look like containers. It seemed weird at first. I arrived with time to spare. I hate being late, so I attempt to make room for unexpected delays. The problem with being early is that you have to wait. I can't explain the emotions and thoughts that tumbled through my mind and body while I waited.

Eventually, I was called. The nurses were kind and gentle. I was having a contrast scan, which meant they needed to insert a cannula into my arm and inject dye into my bloodstream. As I lay on the cold metal bed, I felt the dye surge through my body—a strange, almost unsettling sensation. For a moment, it felt like I was going to wet myself. But of course, I didn't.

Then they slid the bed under the doughnut-shaped scanner and asked me to hold my breath. In what felt like mere seconds, the scan was complete. Quick. Painless. Almost too easy. It seemed impossible that something so simple could be looking for something so terrifying inside me.

Lying there, I was suddenly very thankful for medical technology and advancements.

As I walked out of the room, I found myself searching the faces of the technologists and nurses, hoping for a clue, a sign—anything that might reveal what they had seen. But I knew I couldn't ask.

Because even if I had, they wouldn't have told me.

1 November–12 November 2023 Macmillan Cancer Website

I joined the Macmillan Cancer Support website, and I'm so glad I did. Users create nicknames so they remain anonymous. This allows them to express their deepest feelings without fear of judgment or personal recrimination. There's a comforting anonymity in that—an emotional safety net in a space where everyone understands.

Through this platform, I've been able to follow the journeys of others—people facing something similar. But even with shared experiences, I realise now that no two cancer journeys are ever the same.

Visit: www.macmillan.org.uk for more information about this amazing society.

On this website, I came across a sentence that hit me like a truth I hadn't yet found words for: "*It is the knowing, not knowing, that is the hardest.*"

I couldn't have said it better myself.

This limbo—this waiting between diagnosis and the big questions—all makes the waiting excruciating. "How far has it spread? What's the treatment plan? What comes next?" Right then, at that stage of the journey, limbo felt like the hardest part.

Of course, I knew there might be more difficult days ahead. I knew that I'd maybe look back and realise that this wasn't even the hardest part at all.

But then, it was.

My MRI was booked for 13 November; my next doctor's appointment was on 16 November.

And so I waited.

One cancer sufferer described her emotions as yo-yoing—swinging between normality and uncontrollable sobbing, back and forth, over and over.

I heard her. I understood her.

But I was not experiencing that at all.

Instead, I felt like I was walking on a thin upper crust of complete calmness—a fragile shell of normality. To the outside world, nothing had changed. I went about my days and nights as if cancer had not entered my life.

I mentioned that I've felt more emotions than are listed in the dictionary—but if you were to look at me, you wouldn't know. You'd see only the calm exterior. The thin upper crust.

My fear?

That one day, it would crack. And when it did, I had no idea what would happen.

Beneath this surface, there was fear.

And disbelief.

And more fear.

And anger.

And faith.

And fear again.

It was a warboel of emotions.

I love that Afrikaans word—*warboel*. English words like *chaos*, *confusion*, and *maze* don't quite capture it. *Warboel* feels right. It was a swirling, tangled mess of feelings that refused to settle.

I thought that maybe—just maybe—once I knew exactly what I was dealing with, I could take this warboel of emotions and channel it into something else.

Maybe then I could move from fear to action.

Oh, I forgot to mention something quite irrelevant—not! Mine was an oestrogen-induced cancer. Basically, the hormone replacement therapy (HRT) I'd been on for more than 20 years to manage menopause symptoms caused the cancer. At least the report from the oncologist said that.

When I was in my mid-forties, I started with awful night sweats. I saw my gynaecologist, and she recommended a hysterectomy. She did not remove my ovaries but decided to put me on HRT for the hot flushes and night sweats. I just kept taking the medication, as no doctor told me to stop. At the time of the cancer diagnosis, I was immediately taken off the HRT. The result? The dreaded hot flushes came back with a vengeance.

And let's be clear—I don't get those dainty little *"glows,"* where a light sheen of sweat delicately gathers along the hairline or upper lip.

Oh no, not me.

I get the full-blown, red-hot volcanic eruptions that light me up from the inside and make me want to dive headfirst into a chest freezer and slam the lid shut.

Picture those gas torches—you know, the ones you ignite and they go *whoosh*. Now imagine that happening inside your body. Repeatedly.

You might say, "Well, lucky her! She's in England, and it's winter. So at least it's cold outside."

And yes, you'd be right—except that British homes are basically insulated fortresses. Double glazing? Check. Radiators in every conceivable place? Check. Even in the passage and toilet because God forbid a single draft sneak in.

And let's not forget: If you're caring for the elderly, they feel the cold ten times more. Which means extra heaters cranked up to *tropical rainforest* levels, ensuring that every last hint of fresh air is banished from existence.

Now, if these internal infernos actually melted fat, I might make peace with them.

But nooooooo. They do nothing of the sort.

Bollocks.

Ooh, here comes another one. Gotta go before my sweaty fingers slide right off the keyboard!

PS Calm upper crust was still intact . . . then.

13 November 2023
MRI Day

The MRI was at the same place as the CT scan. I was early and waited, but not for long. The nurses were, as usual, kind and thoughtful. They explained exactly what they were going to do. I needed to whip out the offensive left boob—and the other one, which had done nothing wrong—and place them into two holes on a metal bed. So I lay on my tummy (which I don't particularly like) with my boobs in these holes. I think we need beach lounges like this!

They needed to do a contrast screening, which required them to inject a dye into my vein to enhance the images and make abnormalities more visible.

These nurses were so adept at finding a vein. I was suitably impressed because I have the most elusive veins on the planet.

The vein was quickly found, the dye injected, and the screening performed. All painless.

I packed away my offensive lefty and poor righty, then left. As I departed, I again scanned the faces of the technicians, but they were not giving anything away.

15 November 2023
Plans

Earlier in 2023, I had booked a flight and planned to spend three days in Turkey, then go on to Johannesburg, South Africa, for a month. The main reason? To celebrate my sister Erika's sixtieth birthday.

As a side note, travel is my passion. I love flying. I love visiting other countries and seeing how others live. I love trying different cuisines. I love the beach, and I love thrilling adventures.

Since starting work as a carer, I've been able to do some travelling and enjoy awesome adventures. Paragliding in Mozambique. Swimming with turtles in Zanzibar. Doing a road trip from Florida to Cape Cod with my son. To mention just a few. I love it!

Now, my oncologist wasn't exactly happy about this plan to visit South Africa. "You really shouldn't go," he said.

But I had to.

I needed my family.

I needed their love, their hugs, their smiles, their support.

I needed to be with people who knew me before the word *cancer* entered my life. People who would focus on me more than my disease and the reason for its existence.

Let's pause here for a moment. As I mentioned previously, the HRT caused my cancer. Whenever someone is diagnosed with cancer, people seem desperate to find a reason.

"Oh, she smoked. That's why she has cancer."

"Oh, he drank too much. That's why he got sick."

It's almost as if cancer is some kind of punishment for bad choices. And that if people simply know which bad choices to avoid, they can protect themselves from *the disease.* When my dad was diagnosed with tongue cancer, the first thing people asked was, "Did he smoke?" Because you know—gotta have a reason.

But here's the thing: Cancer doesn't always work that way.

Yes, some lifestyle choices increase your risk. But cancer isn't always about something you *did* or *didn't do*. Sometimes, it just happens. Google it, and you'll learn that our bodies' cells are always growing, dividing, and dying—it's called apoptosis. Damaged cells inevitably appear during this process, but they usually fix themselves or die off naturally. Cancer happens when they don't follow that script. Lifestyle can factor into it, but so does the environment, one's own genetics, or aging. That's the kicker—the body's ability to eliminate damaged cells decreases with age, which is why cancer risk increases as we get older.

So if you are battling cancer or love someone who is, please don't blame anyone. It just adds unnecessary stress. And if there's one thing you don't need when fighting cancer, it's stress.

Chapter 3 – Moving Back to South Africa

16 November 2023
Visit to My Oncologist for Results and a Treatment Plan

It was time to see my oncologist and get some idea of what lay ahead.

The waiting room at the breast clinic was becoming a very familiar place—a place where I sat and waited to see professionals who had answers to my questions and hope for my despair.

Unfortunately, the appointment was “incomplete” (the doctor’s word), as he had not yet received the MRI results. He did say that I could go home to South Africa in December. Nothing was going to stop me. His only concern was that he could not operate for at least six weeks after an international flight. Therefore, he was thinking the surgery would be mid-February. However, there was absolutely nothing definite yet, as I still had to have an ultrasound biopsy on the following Monday. I was hoping that once we got the results from the biopsy, I would have more information.

17 November 2023
Starting a New Drug

On this date, I was prescribed and started taking letrozole tablets every day. As I was going to South Africa and, therefore, treatment in the UK would have to wait, my doctors decided to immediately start me on this drug.

Letrozole lowers the levels of the female sex hormone oestrogen. Oestrogen stimulates some breast cancers—hormone-sensitive or hormone receptor-positive cancers—to grow. This is what I had. Letrozole (and tamoxifen, as I found out later) can stop or slow the growth of these cancers. Unfortunately, one of the common side effects of letrozole is hot flushes.

I have been trying to think how on earth I would put into words what a hot flush feels like.

I remember when Samantha and I were in Dubai for a week. We stayed at The Palm Hotel—a very elegant, gorgeous hotel. Anyway, it was beautifully cool and refreshing inside the hotel. But as we opened the door to go to the swimming pools, our glasses immediately misted up as the hot, humid air hit us. You can imagine how sweat glands expand and release moisture all over your body till you are shining!

Now, a hot flush has a similar result; however, it starts on the inside. It makes no difference what the temperature is on the outside. You just feel this heat bubble up from inside your belly, move up through your chest, and explode into your face. And *every* sweat gland explodes and expels moisture . . . and I mean every sweat gland. Even my hands shine! I am not sure how long it lasts, but I guess about two to three minutes. But they feel like hours. And don't get me started on the night sweats! Duvet is on, and then it is completely off. Then I get cold as the hot flush dissipates and the sweat cools.

27 November 2023
Biopsy Time Again

The MRI found the lump in the left breast. Originally, the doctors took a biopsy from the lump under my arm. The lump in my breast was small and could not be seen clearly in the mammograms or CT scan. Now that the MRI had found the lump, they needed to biopsy it. So I was back at the breast clinic—back in my extremely familiar waiting room, which was starting to feel like my second home!

I was called through to the ultrasound room, and the memories of the first visit came flooding back—memories of thoughts that I just might have cancer. Now I knew I did have cancer.

The doctor was lovely—a lady this time—and she was friendly and gentle and kind. I was back on the hard bed, naked from the waist up (this was becoming the norm) with my arms above my head. She took the biopsy and left a marker in place from where she took it. I left with a large plaster on my left boob.

At this stage, I must tell you that I was really unhappy with "lefty," as I call my left boob. She had let me down. She was carrying an alien, offensive thing. On the other hand, I was thankful that she had let me know there was a problem. So I was having a love/hate relationship with lefty!

In the meantime, I received a letter from the breast clinic that confirmed the following:

> It is a Grade 2 invasive ductal carcinoma ER 7/8 (means hormone oestrogen sensitive),

> PR7/8 (means progesterone sensitive) and HER2 negative (means less aggressive than positive). They have also confirmed that the cancer in the lymph gland is the secondary cancer and therefore assuming the primary is in the breast. The mammogram and the ultrasound did not show any disease in the breast; however, the MRI shows a cyst/lump in the breast measuring 1.5cm and this is what they needed to biopsy.

All the technical terms—which I googled, by the way, to see what they meant—made the cancer seem emotionless (not sure if this is the best way to describe it). Instead, it seemed like a thing with technical medical terms that needed to be dealt with. It sort of put it out there and not in me. Does that make sense?

Only when I used the words *lump* and *cancer* did it become a scary thing.

Receiving the actual technical diagnoses helped me put things into perspective and determine that this was not a death sentence. That it was definitely treatable. It also made me realise that there was a difficult journey ahead

28 November 2023–13 December 2023 On My Way Home: South Africa

I wanted to get home, so I cancelled my three days in Turkey and flew straight to Johannesburg. I arrived home on 29 November 2023. Looking back, I realise I wasn't well at all. I was constantly tired, and I think I was getting depressed.

The past few weeks had been a whirlwind of emotions, decisions, and uncertainty, and I had to go through it all alone. When I landed in South Africa, I was immediately wrapped in the warmth of family—exactly what my emotionally charged self needed. The familiar love, the laughter, the late-night card games, and the simple joy of reminiscing made me realise just how much I had longed for this.

I hadn't cried yet. But when my daughter hugged me, I felt the floodgates threatening to open. She is my rock—kind, practical, loving—and though I didn't know it then, she would become even more important in the months to come.

A few days later, we flew to George—a delightful town along the Garden Route—for Erika's sixtieth birthday and spent a wonderful week in Sedgefield surrounded by friends. We laughed and ate and swam (it was a really sweltering summer) and played games.

Such fun. But I often withdrew—I was definitely getting depressed. I was also extremely tired and getting the most awful hot flushes. I believe stopping the HRT and starting on the letrozole led to these extreme hot flushes. Hot flushes are a common side effect of letrozole and very similar to menopause symptoms that include hot flushes, sweating, and sleep disturbances. The hot flushes, combined with temperatures in the high thirties—typical South African summers—were difficult to deal with.

14 December 2023
Call from the UK Breast Clinic

Then came the call from the UK. A doctor and a nurse were on the line, and they asked me if I had support with me. My darling sister joined me, and we had the call on speaker so all could hear.

The biopsy results confirmed that the primary cancer was in my breast, and surgery was scheduled for 8 January in the UK. But both my doctor and breast care nurse emphasised how much support I would need, as it would be a long journey of treatments.

There would first be a lumpectomy and axillary dissection (meaning lymph node removal). Once I had healed from the operation, I would need at least 16 chemotherapy treatments. Then I would need radiation. They urged me to stay in South Africa if I didn't have the help I needed in the UK. Erika insisted that I stay with her. So it was decided that I would remain in South Africa for all my treatments. All my reports were sent from the National Health Service in the UK to the medical team in South Africa. After the holiday season, I would see a doctor to determine the next steps.

Medical Aid in South Africa

I want to mention something unbelievable. In January 2023, I decided to take out a medical aid in South Africa for those times when I visited home. It is good to have a medical aid because you don't really want to be in a government hospital in South Africa. You pay a monthly fee towards the medical aid, and depending on the cover you have chosen, your medical treatments will be covered by the medical aid. Cancer is what they call a "prescribed minimum benefit," which means that the medical aid will cover most of the cancer treatments required. Having a medical aid allows you to see private doctors and hospitals, which, as I mentioned, is much better in South Africa. The government hospitals are not well run. Little did I know in January 2023 how much I would need that medical aid from January 2024 on. It was good and covered so much of my treatment that was to come. I will always be grateful that I had it.

I felt immense relief that I would be close to Erika, my daughter Sam, and their spouses. When you are vulnerable, you definitely need loving family and friends to support you. Don't be afraid to ask.

I don't ask for help easily. During a difficult marriage, whenever my husband asked the children to do something, I would interrupt and say, "Don't worry. I will do it!" My reaction was due to my husband's volatile temper, which could explode at any time. I didn't want my children to bear the brunt of it, if possible. My mom eventually said she was going to put this on my gravestone: "Don't worry. I'll do it." So after doing it myself for 27 married years, I still battle to ask for help.

My children call me stubborn because I always want to do it myself. But this journey made me realise that when I truly need help, I should just ask.

By nature, I am a very capable person. And doing things myself kept the peace in the home. Besides, asking for help and then not receiving it is far too painful to deal with.

15 December–23 December 2023 A Blissful Trip Along the Garden Route and Visiting Precious Friends

On my trip, I visited a lot of people from different times in my life, and it gave me courage. It was also wonderful to reconnect, reminisce, and just enjoy renewed friendships together.

My sister and her hubby flew back to Pretoria, and I spent two days in Knysna with Irene, my travel buddy. We floated in the river, chatted, explored markets, and simply soaked in the peaceful moments. She and I had booked a walking holiday on the Amalfi Coast through Walk About Italy. We should have done it in 2023, but Irene's passport was stolen on a flight from South Africa to London. So we postponed to 2024, not knowing, of course, what lay ahead for me. Thanks to my diagnosis, I was unsure if the trip would happen in 2024. After spending time in Knysna, I drove to Stilbaai, where I spent two nights with my dear friend Rita, who gave me a place to rest. One evening, with deep respect and quiet sadness, I scattered Aunt Bea's ashes. Aunt Bea was my mother's sister. She never married, and she was like a second mum to us. She died while I was in the UK, and I could not be at her bedside or attend her funeral, so scattering her ashes was my goodbye to her. It was a difficult but necessary goodbye, and I was grateful to have Rita by my side.

Next, I went to Hermanus, where I spent time with Carl and Caroline—great company, tasty food, and meaningful conversations. The following day, I took the scenic coastal drive to Cape Town. It was breathtaking. I stopped often, allowing myself the luxury of taking it all in. Driving alone meant I could go at my own pace, with no agenda but mine. I needed that.

I had a lovely, comfortable hire car with an excellent air conditioner. Thank goodness because the hot flushes were getting worse and worse.

In Cape Town, I enjoyed a beautiful reunion with friends and family. Cape Town is also my favourite city, with its beautiful beaches, pristine white sand and sparkling blue water, majestic mountains—especially Table Mountain—vineyards, and scenic drives. It is just breathtaking beauty everywhere you look. It is also the city I grew up, so revisiting the places of my childhood held a special kind of nostalgia.

I caught up with Gwen, who—no matter how much time passes—makes me feel like I saw her only yesterday. I stayed with Jacques and Jeni, two of the most wonderful, loving people I know. Their grandson is possibly the most beautiful little boy I've ever seen (besides, of course, my own son!).

One of the highlights of my time in Cape Town was the Red Bus Tour. Jeni, Jacques, and I hopped on at the V&A Waterfront, wound through the city, stopped at Kirstenbosch for a walk along the Tree Canopy Walkway, then headed to Hout Bay for the best fish and chips. Sitting on the top deck of the bus, free from the stress of traffic, I could fully appreciate the beauty of the Mother City. I can recommend this trip to all tourists in Cape Town. That evening, we braaied (barbecued) with Sean, Kerry, and little Levi—a night filled with love and laughter.

I also met up with Muriel—another dear friend—and my stepsister Colleen. I spent one special evening at Eden on the Bay—an unforgettable meal, a spectacular sunset, and, for once, a windless Cape Town night (a rare blessing!). Of course, the next day, the southeasterly wind returned, draping Table Mountain in its signature tablecloth.

24 December 2023–1 January 2024 Erika's Actual Sixtieth and Christmas Day

After Cape Town, I flew back to Johannesburg to spend Christmas with Erika and her husband Pieter.

I wanted to be there for her actual birthday on 24 December and celebrate Christmas surrounded by family. Family has always been important to me, but facing illness makes you see it in an entirely different light.

Physically, I struggled. There were moments I wanted to collapse from sheer exhaustion, but I pushed through, determined to make the most of this trip. Now I was finally allowing myself to rest and listen to what my body needed.

The three of us celebrated New Year with a delicious potjie done on the fire. A potjie is like a stew done in a cast iron pot and cooked on an open fire. Something us South Africans love! At that time, I was glad that I didn't know what was lying ahead.

It's astonishing how life can change so completely in just a few months.

Chapter 4 – Treatment Begins

2 January 2024
GP Visit

I visited my GP on 2 January. He has been my GP for many years and knows my medical history, so I wanted to see him and tell him of my cancer diagnosis. I thought I might need him during my cancer treatments, so I wanted him to know I was in South Africa for a while. At the consultation, he discovered that my blood sugar was 16.3 and recommended a sugar fast test for the next day. That test was 12. This meant I was diabetic. He put me on metformin and diaglucide, medications to control blood sugar. Just another curveball that I didn’t expect.

4 January 2024
Oncologist Visit

I had my first meeting with the oncologist at the nearby hospital.

Erika came with me to be my cancer buddy, my support system, and the ears I knew I'd need. Erika and Sam were there for me every step of the way. When you're hit with so many emotions, it's hard to take in all the medical info, so having them with me was such a comfort.

The oncologist examined me and then took out a piece of paper to draw a timeline of the treatment plan. I added my own notes and dates so I could begin to understand how long this journey might be. According to his timeline, I'd finish radiation on 31 August 2024. Nearly *eight months* of treatment.

That hit hard. I had imagined I'd be done by May. But no—end of August was now my new target, and I had to adjust my mindset. I didn't know then that even August wouldn't be the finish line. Treatments would stretch closer to December.

The treatment plan started with a lumpectomy and lymph node removal, which they call an axillary dissection. Then when I was healed from the operation, they would start chemotherapy. The chemo is called

AC—nicknamed the "Red Devil"—with four treatments spaced 21 days apart. AC chemotherapy is a chemotherapy regimen that combines two drugs called doxorubicin (or Adriamycin) and cyclophosphamide. After that would come 12 weekly treatments of another chemotherapy drug called paclitaxel. Then once chemo ended, I'd move on to four weeks of daily radiation. And finally, I'd be taking an oestrogen-suppressing drug for the next five to ten years. At the same time, my oncologist took me off the letrozole tablet.

I received one very important warning while receiving chemotherapy: If my temperature went above 38°C between days five and ten after chemo, I must contact the hospital immediately. It could mean infection, and my immune system wouldn't be able to fight any infection on its own.

This was my path. It was longer than I'd expected. It was heavier than I'd imagined. But with my team, my cancer buddies, my family and support, and a fierce will to fight, I was walking it one step at a time.

15 January 2024
Rambling Thoughts

The temperature today was around 35°C! And then, every hour or so, the fire would ignite in my chest and spread throughout my body. I would end up red and wet! My darling sister bought me a spray bottle, which we filled with ice water. It brought relief for a short while but relief, nonetheless. They say you can apply antiperspirant to your hairline to assist with the sweat! Yes, I tried it all . . .

I don't know how anyone could live with me during this time because my emotions were all over the place. I was weary beyond words and sometimes depressed. Other times, I was chatty and laughing, then moody. My poor family. All I can say is thank you for putting up with me.

17 January 2024
Your Health

I saw a dietitian to help me with the diabetes. I needed a professional to guide me and help me make wiser food choices. All I can say is, if you are healthy and are reading this, *please look after your health.* Bad health affects every aspect of your life . . . every aspect. Hopefully, it isn't too late for me.

My thought was to get through the cancer treatment and apply myself to healthy eating and gentle exercise. Slowly but surely, I hoped to gain my strength again.

Irene and I had booked our Amalfi walk for September 2024, so I had a goal and needed to apply myself so we could thoroughly enjoy that holiday.

Little did I know in January that I would just be finishing my chemo by September 2024, so the Amalfi walk definitely didn't happen in 2024. Maybe 2025!

18 January 2024
Visit to the Surgeon

In many of the books and memoirs I have read about breast cancer, surgery happens after chemotherapy. Strange, but I never asked my oncologist why he wanted the surgery first.

On 18 January, my daughter left me a little message in my diary: "I heart you." It warmed my heart. One of my mother's favourite sayings was "Kindness never leaves a scar. Only an impression." So true.

So I found myself in the surgeon's waiting room with Erika—my stomach full of knots. I was so glad I had Erika with me. My oncologist had told me the surgeon would only do a lumpectomy and not a mastectomy. In other words, only the lump in my left breast would be removed. He would also need to remove lymph nodes under my arm because the secondary cancer was in the lymph glands.

After a short wait, we were ushered into the surgeon's consulting room. He was a really nice man, friendly and kind. He examined me and confirmed it would be a lumpectomy and axillary dissection and that I would only need to be at a day hospital. They would operate in the morning, and I would go home in the evening. Awesome!

I very strangely looked forward to the operation. I wanted the cancer removed from my body as soon as possible. I hated knowing there was this evil lurking in me and destroying me from the inside. I hated wondering where it would spread to next. I just wanted it out.

29 January 2024
Lumpectomy and Axillary Dissection (Lymph Node Removal)

On 29 January, my sister and I were on our way to the hospital. It was a beautiful summer morning in Pretoria. I could feel that it would be another muggy day, with temperatures soaring into the thirties. I love hearing the birds early in the morning. To me, they seem happy and excited that it is a new day. On this day, they were encouraging me to feel the same, but it wasn't easy.

This was the day for the alien lump in my lefty and my lymph nodes to be removed. I couldn't wait. I hated the thought of this nasty "thing" invading and residing inside me. I wanted it out, and I wanted it out now.

We arrived at the hospital at the same time as the surgeon. In fact, we rode up the escalator together! So everything happened pretty quickly. The nurses got me dressed for theatre in those cute pants you wear. They always make us laugh. It distracted me a bit from what was soon to happen.

As much as I wanted this operation and the removal of this offensive lump, I was still scared. I worried about it having spread further and thought about pain. Fortunately, as I said, I was wheeled to the theatre very quickly, as the surgeon was waiting. There was no more time to think. Now it was time to sleep!

I woke up after the operation with an awful pain on my left side, then called out for help. A lovely nurse gave me pain medication, and I drifted off back to sleep. When I opened my eyes again, I saw Erika. (Such a blessing!) My darling daughter came to the hospital to take over from my sister. How lucky I am to have them love and care for me.

I had a drain, which was a pain . . . ooh, that rhymes! The drain came out of the wound where they removed the lymph nodes. Fluid draining from a wound after surgery is a common occurrence and a normal part of healing. I was instructed to measure the fluid each time I emptied it, as the surgeon would remove it only once most of the fluid had drained.

Late that afternoon, I was told I could go home to recover.

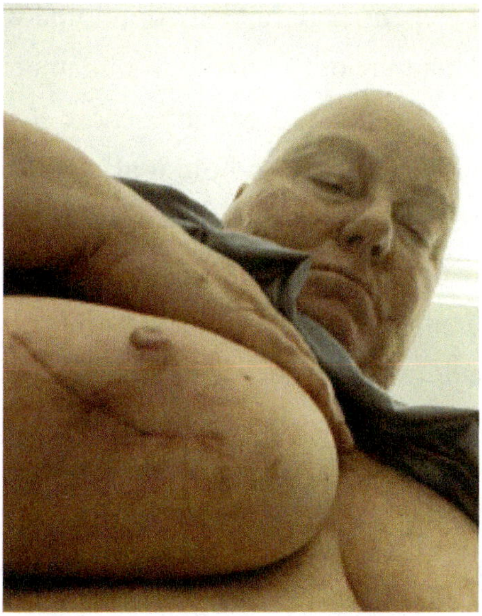

Lumpectomy wound.

30 January 2024
So Thankful for Family Help

My daughter came to help me shower every day. What would I have done without Sam? She is gentle, kind, and loving, and I feel completely comfortable with her. What a blessing to have such an amazingly wonderful daughter. Thank you, my precious girl, for all you did for me and all you mean to me.

It was difficult to shower, as I could not get the dressings wet and had this long drainpipe with a bag at the end hanging out from the wound under my arm. It was painful when it dropped because it yanked in the wound, so I needed to hold it all the time. When I was dressed, I slipped it into my knickers! I knew knickers would come in handy someday! Disgusting fluid drained from the wound and into the bag at the end of the drainpipe. I needed to measure it and empty it into the toilet every now and again. Just another awful task I hadn't expected.

Erika took me to my appointment with the surgeon and his nurse so they could change the dressing and check the drain. The drain was really not nice.

Here, I must just say thank you again to Sam for helping me. The roles reversed, and my daughter became the one who cared tenderly for her mother. I can't put into words what it means to me. Thinking about it always tends to make me well up with a deep love and thankfulness for my children. They are both my reason for living.

I developed an awful blister, just to add to the need for more dressings. Then I got an infection on the incision on my boob, which needed antibiotics. I slept in a La-Z-Boy chair for about eight days after the operation, which put my body in the perfect position to support my arm.

The surgeon removed eight lymph nodes—two were malignant. And then, of course, he removed the lump in the offensive lefty. The lymph node incision was way more painful and uncomfortable. After the operation, I was chatting to a plastic surgeon who is a friend, and he was not happy that my surgeon had removed eight lymph nodes if only two were malignant. Apparently, you can inject dye into the lump in the breast, and it will go towards the malignant nodes. That way, the surgeon needs to remove only the cancerous ones.

Lymph nodes have an important function. They act as filters for the lymphatic system, trapping and destroying foreign substances like bacteria, viruses, and cancer cells. They also play a crucial role in fluid balance by returning excess interstitial fluid to the bloodstream. The top of my arm was "dead," but every now and again, as the nerves tried to mend, I experienced what felt like shots of electricity or hectic pins and needles. It's hard to explain. It wasn't too painful—more of a weird, uncomfortable sensation. As I write this more than a year later, the outside of my upper arm is still completely numb. In fact, if I were into tattoos, it would be the ideal place to get one because I wouldn't feel them doing it!

At this stage, however, I was so happy to report that all dressings had been removed, as well as the drain, as the wounds were healing well. And *best of all*, I could swim! It had been *so* hot, and I could go into the pool only up to my waist to cool off. That first night after all the dressings were removed, I stayed in the pool for a long time. It was wonderful. As the sun set and the trees cast long shadows over the swimming pool and I floated on my back, I felt the stress leave my body. It dissolved into the swimming pool water and left me weightless. No more dressings. No more cancer—or so I thought at the time!

My next appointment with the oncologist was going to be Monday, 12 February. Then I would find out how he was going to proceed with chemotherapy and radiation.

Emotionally, I was a bit of a wreck. I swung from feeling smiley, happy, and positive one minute to quiet, depressed, and sad the next. It was like flipping a switch, and I couldn't control it. I was also so tired—exhausted in ways I can't explain.

Erika and I did some shopping for her work, and it was great to get out and feel normal for a bit. But then, out of the blue, a hot flush hit, and everything changed. I was instantly wiped out. I couldn't keep my eyes open or my feet moving. My heart started racing, and I felt lightheaded, like I was going to faint right there in the store. It was overwhelming, and I just wanted to collapse.

But then there were other times when I felt okay. Not great, not perfect, but okay. It's strange. It was like my body could go from one extreme to the other in an instant, and I never knew what I was going to get.

Definition of fatigue: "A persistent feeling of tiredness or exhaustion that doesn't go away with rest. It can affect your physical, mental, and emotional well-being, making it difficult to perform daily activities and concentrate."

I can't say it any better than this!

To go from a fairly healthy, active 64-year-old woman to someone who was extremely unwell was deeply humbling, frightening, and heartbreaking. It's hard to explain how jarring it is to lose the strength and independence I once took for granted. This shift shook me to my core.

What's hardest wasn't just the physical illness. It was the emotional weight.

The vulnerability.

The loss of control.

The feeling that my body no longer reflected the person I'd always been.

It was scary not knowing what was next.

12 February 2024
Second Visit to the Oncologist

It was time to see my oncologist and start with the chemotherapy treatment plan he had laid out.

I was scheduled for four chemotherapy treatments starting 19 February, all spaced 21 days apart. That plan would take me through to 22 April. After that, I expected to have a different chemotherapy every week for 12 weeks. These sessions would end by 29 July. And then the doctors planned another four weeks of radiation, which they said should wrap up by 31 August.

Just typing this made my hands shake.

I was scared. Not just of what this was doing to my body but of everything it was taking from me.

The time.

The energy,

The ability to work.

The stability I'd always fought to hold onto.

As a financial planner, I know all too well how critical insurance is. But sadly, I didn't have coverage.

No safety net. Nothing to fall back on.

Little did I know then that the above treatment plan's time frame was way off. I'll tell you more later.

Chapter 5 – Chemotherapy, Round 1

19 February 2024
Chemotherapy Starts

When I couldn't sleep at night because my mind was one warboel of thoughts and emotions, I would think that when morning came, I'd put all these thoughts into words so I could calm my mind!

I had a port just under my right shoulder so the nurses would have access to my veins. (This was inserted during the lumpectomy because I have extremely elusive veins.) I applied some numbing cream when I got dressed that morning, hoping I would hardly feel them insert the needle to administer all the drugs.

I had to have blood taken before every chemo appointment. They checked the red and white blood cell count as well as some other numbers to make sure I was strong enough to handle the chemo.

Once the nurses had inserted the IV tubes into the port, they took me into the chemo room, where I slid into the nearest empty La-Z-Boy chair and surrendered myself to the drugs. Darling Erika stayed with me till then but had to leave, as there wasn't room for each patient to have a chemo buddy sitting with them.

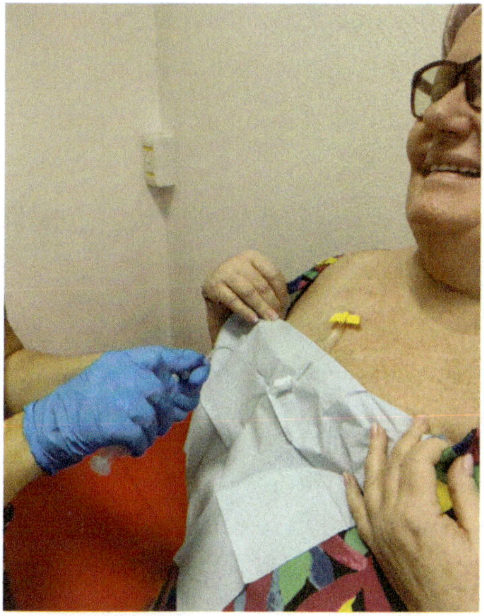

Nurse inserting the needle and tube into the port for the first chemo.

It was strange to be there at last. There were all these La-Z-Boy chairs lined up next to each other and back-to-back. Someone was sitting in each one, attached to a drip. Some were reading, some were sleeping, some were listening to something through their earphones, and some were chatting to each other. Most had no hair or were wearing wigs or some sort of headgear. I was a newbie and viewed everything with interest. I hoped they could see on my face that I was not really one for conversation. They probably also saw the terror on my face, although I tried to hide it. I had a book to read but was also open to just lying back and closing my eyes!

The nurses were wonderful and explained everything to me as they went along. They first gave me three different bags of anti-nausea medication and cortisone. Each took about ten to fifteen minutes to run in. Then there were two bags of chemo meds called AC. A is doxorubicin (also called Adriamycin), and C is cyclophosphamide. These each take about 30 minutes. They call this chemo the Red Devil! This is the chemo drug that causes your hair to fall out. It also causes extreme fatigue and many other side effects.

Let me share some of the side effects so you can understand why most cancer patients fear this chemo drug. Common side effects are hair loss, nausea, vomiting, mouth sores, fatigue, and changes in blood counts. It lowers white blood cell counts, increasing the risk of infection, and platelets, leading to an increased risk of bleeding and bruising. Therefore, I believe the name "Red Devil" is apt. Besides the fact that it is red.

Normally, with any illness, you don't know you are going to get sick. You just wake up one morning and you are sick—let's say with chicken pox as an example. You then see the doctor and get medication, and you deal with the consequences of chicken pox. But this doesn't apply with chemo.

While the meds were dripping into my veins, a nurse brought me a 14-page A4 document listing all the side effects and proceeded to highlight the most important and dangerous ones (as per above).

I knew beforehand that I could get these side effects, and this played havoc with my mind and emotions. Every twinge, every pain, every sensation—well, just about everything I felt—made me panic. I became tuned in and aware of my body. I guess it was important to know what could happen, but I also felt that not knowing would be more peaceful.

While the drugs were running into me, another sweet nurse came to me with two hats and asked which one I would like. She said they were free and that I would need them because I would be bald when I came back in three weeks! That was a bit of a shock. I didn't realise it happens so quickly.

When I was still reeling from that realisation, the nurses disconnected me from the IV and released me from the recliner. I wished I could go home, but unfortunately, I needed to go upstairs to see my surgeon. I had developed a seroma under my left arm where the lymph glands were removed. A seroma is basically a swelling—a buildup of fluid under the skin after surgery or any trauma. Apparently, it is a common complication, especially after breast surgery and plastic surgery. My surgeon sent me to the radiologists to have the fluid drained from the seroma. They drained 200 ml but could not get it all out, as the needle wasn't long enough. They told me that my body should absorb the rest. Then they sent the fluid to pathology for testing, so I would need to wait for those results.

Before leaving, I was given a medication called olanzapine and instructed to take it the first five nights after chemo. I learned it was a schizophrenia treatment, which frightened me. But the doctor told me that it's also prescribed to chemo patients to prevent nausea.

Finally, after two hours, it was time to go home.

My afternoon was a bit uncomfortable with nausea and a dull headache no painkiller could cure. I managed a game of Scrabble with my sis—and she beat me! Then, around nine p.m., I took an olanzapine tablet. I was restless and could not sleep. I met up with Erika in the lounge just before midnight and watched some TV, then tried again. Thankfully, I then slept till five a.m.

26 February 2024
Not an Easy Day

I didn't suffer from too much nausea or headache in the week following my first chemo appointment. I napped more and ate less, but I was grateful for that—I needed to lose some weight! However, I developed the most awful, painful, burning reflux I had ever experienced in my life. I cannot tell you just how excruciatingly painful it was. It was a sharp pain radiating from my front to my back. I called the oncologist in desperation, and he immediately prescribed what I would in the future call a magic drug: Trustan. It relieved the pain within two days. I was thankful beyond words. It's strange how just the smallest things could help make my days better.

I again developed a seroma under my left arm. And again, I had to go to the radiologist's office to have it drained. This time, the radiologist said there was also a buildup of fluid on my left breast. He drained that fluid as well and sent it off to pathology.

Several days later, I again had a buildup of fluid under my arm. This time, the surgeon asked me to come to his practice so he could examine me. So my sister and I went to the surgeon again. He checked my wounds and the seroma, then looked at the pathology reports and told me that there was nothing to worry about. The fluid taken from the breast was clear. The fluid taken from the lymph nodes had cancer cells, but he said that was normal. I had to let my body absorb that fluid and not have it drained again. He really made it sound as if a few cancer cells in the lymph node area were nothing to worry about, as my body would absorb the fluid. To this day, I can't explain why I wasn't more concerned about that.

On my way out, I asked the nurse for the pathology reports, as I was gathering all documentation to take back to England. I would have to see my oncologist there for the follow-up treatment plan once all was completed in South Africa.

Erika and I got in the car, and I started to read the reports. I read and read again. And then again. I thought, *It can't be true!* The surgeon had it wrong.

The fluid drained from the lymph nodes was clear, but the fluid drained from the breast had malignant cells.

I was absolutely horrified. How on earth did this doctor get it so wrong? I didn't know if I should scream from anger or cry from heartache. How did he miss this? He had removed the original cancer source—the lump in my breast—but had not managed to get it all out. Now there was cancer in the fluid in my breast.

What now? Why?

Erika and I discussed it all the way home. I was glad that I had her to share this with. It would have been a difficult burden to carry alone.

Once we were home, I contacted my surgeon friend, Roger, and sent him the pathology reports. He was just as shocked as I was. His advice was immediate: a mastectomy.

It felt like a gut punch!

I had already gone through surgery. I had already started chemotherapy. And now, everything had to be put on hold—paused—while the surgeon and oncologist determined the best path forward.

To be completely honest, I had only one thought at that point: *Just take it. Remove this offensive breast as quickly as possible.*

I didn't stop to consider how I would look. I didn't think about what it might mean for my femininity, my identity, or my sense of self.

I didn't think at all.

I just wanted it gone.

Roger called a surgeon friend of his and managed to make an appointment for me for 11 March.

That night, I had the worst vomiting fit you can imagine. It felt like I was vomiting all my insides out. The noise that came from my throat was frightening. Kneeling at the toilet was painful because I had a bad knee, so Erika brought me a cushion. Luckily, it didn't last too long and didn't happen again. Maybe it was from the shock of the day? I don't know.

1 March 2024
Take Ownership of Your Illness

A few days had passed since I'd relaxed on a comfy La-Z-Boy chair, having "poison" dripped into my veins. I had learned so much in those last few days.

The first and most important lesson is this: Take ownership of your illness. Doctors make mistakes. They are only human. Know what is happening. That includes what you are given and what the side effects could be. Question the doctors if you are unsure.

Someone referred to the chemo treatment as follows: Week one is a black week because it's a really bad week. Week two is a grey week as you start to feel better. Week three is a white week because you start to feel normal again. And then it starts all over again when your next chemo is due.

Honestly, my first week wasn't really black. I only had waves of nausea. And I still had my hair. The worst I had was extreme fatigue and awful heartburn. I did hit a bit of a low, but I think that was due to a doughnut I ate! (I know, I know—I shouldn't have been eating sugary stuff!)

My thought was *Let me just get through the first three weeks*.

I figured that maybe then I'd have a better sense of things and know if there were black, grey, or even some white weeks.

My support structure kept me going. The people around me, along with their love and their encouragement, mattered more than I can say.

But I would be lying if I said I didn't feel like a burden sometimes.

Everyone has hectic lives filled with work, family, and responsibilities. And there I was, needing help, needing time, and needing more than I ever had before.

It was hard to feel so dependent when I'd spent a lifetime being the one who gave support. Not the one needing to ask for it. That shift is painful.

7 March 2024
The Inevitable Hair Loss

Hair falling out in chunks. I see shave day looming!

Can you guess what happened on this day?

Yes, shave day.

I couldn't wait any longer. My hair was falling out in chunks, and it was messy, sticky, hot, and uncomfortable. It was just easier to shave it off. My son-in-law did a video while my daughter slid the electric razor through my hair. She shaved it a number 4, and then a few days later my brother-in-law shaved it a number 1 because it was still falling out. It's pretty messy to have hair on your pillow and headboard all the time. It was also itchy as it fell on my neck. Plus, I was hot.

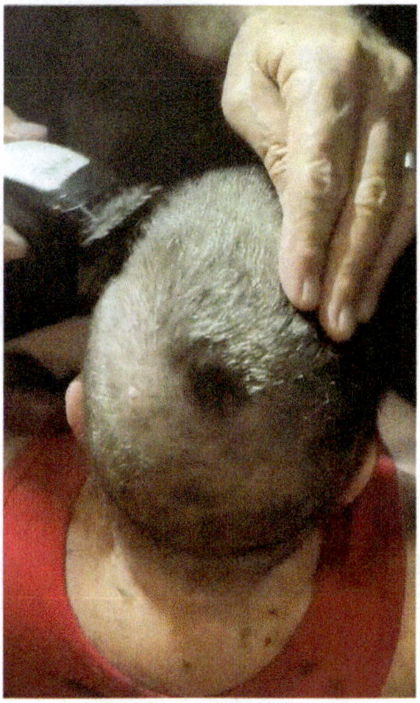

Shave day.

Anyway, it was off. Pieter stood by in solidarity and also had a shave! I appreciated it hugely. We looked like two escaped convicts! I'd tried on some wigs the day before—oh dear, what a disaster! They looked so false, and they were so hot. I decided that I might stick to hats for now.

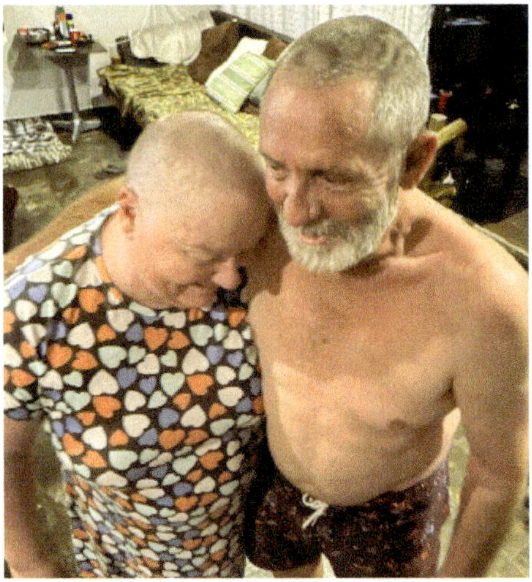

Bandits! Pieter, my brother-in-law, standing by me in solidarity.

Our hair!

Headgear.

Trying on wigs – NO, don't like them!

11 March 2024
Second Chemo Day and the Day to See My New Surgeon

Three weeks passed after my first chemotherapy.

I had never before experienced the mixture of feelings that I was experiencing on this day. I went from sheer panic to tremendous anger and then to sadness. I was scared at times and just wanted to be alone so I could curl up and cry for a while. I often wanted to be alone. And then my spirits would seem to lift, and I could laugh again. I guess you could just call me crazy. My poor family. They didn't know from one moment to the next what mood they were going to get from me. I know I was not easy to live with during all this. Thankfully, they seemed to cope!

When I arrived for my second chemo, my oncologist told me about the results from the pathologists and said he recommended a mastectomy immediately. He would continue chemo only once I had healed from the mastectomy.

Of course, I knew this already. I told him that I had managed to get an appointment that afternoon with a different surgeon. He was relieved. So all chemotherapy treatment was put on hold.

I had spoken to Sam and Erika—as well as my son-in-law and brother-in-law—in these discussions about the mastectomy. *Must I only do the left breast?* I wondered. *Should I remove both?* After much debate, I decided on a double mastectomy. The reason: I didn't want to be bothered with having to wear a bra to support the right breast and then try and stuff the left cup to make it look like I had a boob. Besides, I generally hate bras. Also, what if, in the future, I got cancer in the right breast? It was a risk I didn't want to take. I didn't think I could face this journey again.

From the time we are young, we look in the mirror, judge ourselves, and try to make ourselves look as pretty or handsome as possible. This is the part of us that the world sees. We spend money on creams, lotions, makeup, and clothes—all to look nice. And there is absolutely nothing wrong with that. I think it is important to take care of yourself and make the best of your appearance. But it's strange: When your health is threatened, the focus turns to the inside of the body and not the outward appearance. Don't get me wrong. I still want to look as good as possible. (I guess that is the human pride kicking in.) But if being flat-chested means better health, well, then hell's bells. Take these mammaries off!

So as they say, "Just when I thought it was safe to go back in the water, another shark appeared!"

My appointment with the surgeon Roger recommended was late in the afternoon of the same day I met with my oncologist. Sam went with me for moral support and to help me finally decide. One boob or two? After some debate between the surgeon and his opinion, Sam and her thoughts, and my gut feeling, I finally decided on a double mastectomy. The operation was immediately booked for three days later—14 March. The surgeon told me I was unique (his exact words) as he had never seen cancer cells in a seroma before. My oncologist put it more cautiously by saying that it was most unusual and definitely not normal.

So I would bid farewell to my mammaries. I decided that I might even take a photo of them as a keepsake. Because reconstruction would have delayed chemo, I wasn't able to have it yet. Both the surgeon and oncologist agreed: Starting chemo as soon as possible was vital. So reconstruction would have to wait. And maybe in a year or two, when all treatments were done and dusted, I'd come back and end up with two smaller, perky boobies. How is that for an incentive and positive thinking!

I am being facetious, but I was dreading the next few days and months ahead. I can't lie about that. This Big C negatively affects every aspect of one's life—emotional, physical, mental, and financial.

Chapter 6 – Mastectomy

14 March 2024
Second Surgery: A Double Mastectomy

Oh, it was a real topsy-turvy couple of days.

When 14 March arrived, I had to bid farewell to both of my boobies. I don't know if *bittersweet* is the right word, but it was one of those moments when I really wanted them gone because of the evil they were harbouring. And yet I was sad to see them go because they were part of my femininity. I watched them grow when I was young. They gave me pleasure when I was intimate with a man. My babies suckled on them. They were very much a part of me.

Each weighed about 600 g, so I lost just over a kg! How is that for some positive thinking? I think my mama would have been proud of my finding the positive in the extreme negative!

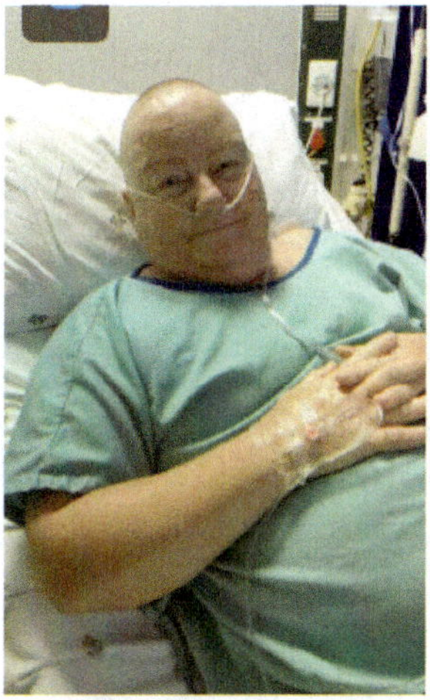

I spent three days in hospital and had two drains and several drips. Just before they released me, the nurses removed one drain. But the other had to stay in. I was now definitely looking like a cancer patient: bald and boobless going home.

Hospitals and I have a long history. This cancer journey wasn't my first dance with doctors, bedsides, and surgical gowns.

My first major surgery came just six days after my daughter was born. During pregnancy or birth, my ascending colon twisted and started to rupture. When the surgeon finally got to it, he told me I had been just two hours from death. I spent three weeks in hospital recovering. My son was almost five, and my newborn daughter had barely opened her eyes. It was a brutal time—emotionally and physically.

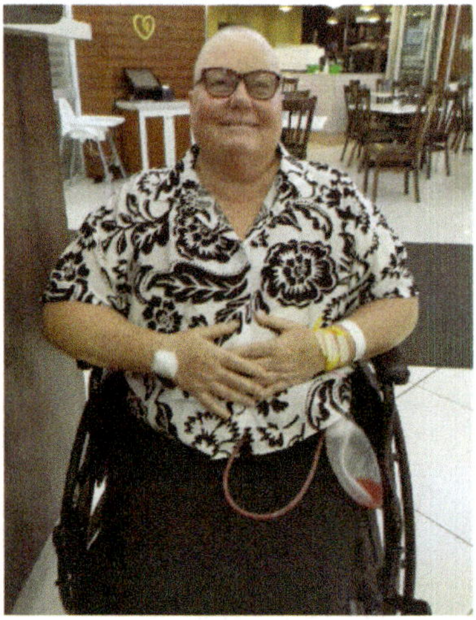

Going home to recover.

The second major surgery was a three-in-one special: a hysterectomy, a bladder lift, and a tummy tuck. (Might as well go all in, right?) It wasn't easy, but I recovered.

Then came the third. A portion of my colon had to be removed due to diverticulitis. That was followed by eight weeks in hospital on and off. I also had a temporary stoma for two months. Then there was a reversal surgery after that. But it didn't end there. I had to be rushed back to hospital three times for bowel blockages. Finally, after what felt like a never-ending storm lasting all of four months, my system settled, and I healed.

I'll never forget one moment. About a week after the surgery, the surgeon came into my hospital room and told me, "There is no cancer in your colon."

And I burst into tears.

He looked confused and said, "But I said there's *no* cancer."

I told him, "That's why I'm crying. I never once thought cancer was even a possibility. Just hearing the word completely shook me."

That moment never left me.

20 March 2024
Surgeon Visit

Six days after the operation, I had to see the surgeon for a wound dressing change. I was also hoping he would remove the offensive, uncomfortable drain. But no luck—it had to stay for another week. During those six days, I was in physical pain and discomfort. Emotionally, I was a wreck. I was exhausted. I don't have words, really. I just took it moment by moment to get through each day. Sam again performed shower duty, but this time, it included wound care.

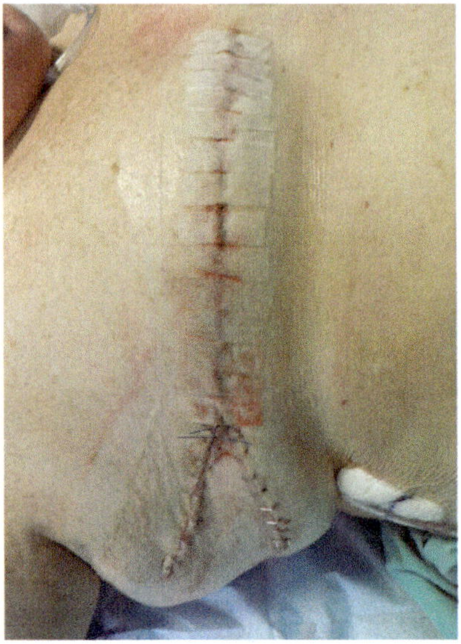

Just after surgery. This is the right boob.

I told the nursing sister at the surgeon's offices how *incredibly* tired I felt. Her response gave me some perspective. She said that after an operation like this in the past, patients spent seven to ten days resting and recovering in hospital. Now, they're sent home much sooner—but a body's healing needs haven't changed. She gently reminded me to do as little as possible and rest as much as I could.

This surgery . . . it's no small thing. I felt like I had a tight band constantly wrapped around my chest, and

I was so swollen under both arms. The fatigue was unlike anything I'd ever felt—and honestly, I struggle to describe it to anyone.

Amid all this, there was one beautiful light: my precious daughter. She came every day to help me bathe. It was such a tender act of care. And in those quiet moments, I felt so loved . . . and, strangely, pampered. What a gift it is to be cared for so gently when everything feels heavy.

A note Erika put on Facebook:

> A little update on my sus, Vren. This evening for the first time, she shared that she is scared. She is worried about what lies ahead. She was in tears, however; Sam and I were there to hold her and hug her. She is incredibly open about everything since the inception of her hearing of the big C. But it makes her human to have given way to her emotions this evening. Strangely though, soon after her tears, we found ourselves laughing about something stupid. Can you believe it was about how a chicken lays eggs! Ok, I won't go into detail (major giggles), but it was funny and between the tears a lot of laughter. I want to thank my sis for being vulnerable,

sharing everything of what she is going through. Thanks to all her friends for your love, kindness and caring. Big hugs to all. I love you stukkend my sis. Big Time

Erika and me in a doctor's waiting room. We spent a lot of time in waiting rooms together!

25 March 2024
The Poison I Was Asking For

It's strange how I hated chemo with everything in me, and yet there I was, wanting it to start again as soon as possible.

I thought, *Please give me the poison that kills the dividing cells in my body. Please give me the poison that brings immense fatigue, horrific heartburn, and waves of nausea.*

How weird is that?

This journey was full of contradictions: The very thing that made me feel awful was also the thing keeping me alive.

It was another topsy-turvy week. I went to see the oncologist, expecting chemo to restart. I had braced myself for it. But instead, I was told that my body was too weak from the mastectomy, so chemotherapy had to still wait.

So now, it was tentatively booked for 11 April. Another twist. Another pause I wasn't ready for.

And I sat with it all—frustration, fatigue, fear, and hope—waiting for the strength to come back. Waiting to begin again.

27 March 2024
Surgeon Visit

Today, I saw my surgeon, and thankfully, they removed the drain. What an incredible relief it was to be free of that tube and the bag that had been constantly hanging from my body. It was always in the way, both physically and emotionally. With them gone, I felt a little more human again.

Unfortunately, the staples and stitches were still in—they'd be removed on 8 April. I didn't want to complain, but honestly . . . it was really uncomfortable and often quite painful. A double mastectomy is no joke. This is not just a physical journey—it's a mental, emotional, and financial one too.

Speaking of which, the medical expenses were piling up. My medical aid didn't cover everything, and the bills just kept coming. To help myself, I started a digital marketing business online. I was doing everything I could to rebuild, support myself, and manage this new chapter of life.

I am so thankful for friends, acquaintances, and family who donated financial aid as well as prayers. Sometimes, they just popped in and checked up on me. They helped carry me in moments when I could not carry myself. Somehow, God always knew when I was in dire need. Just when things seemed impossible and I could not make ends meet, my phone would ping and there would be a small deposit in my account. Sometimes, they were anonymous—a quiet miracle right when I needed it most

Oh—and then there was my bald head.

I'm still getting used to it. Every time I passed a mirror and caught my reflection, I got a little fright. *Who is that strange, fierce-looking woman staring back at me?* I'd wonder. *She looks unfamiliar. But maybe, just maybe, she's braver than I give her credit for.*

I hadn't yet managed to leave the house without something covering my head. I would wear either a scarf, a beanie, or a hat. Thankfully, I love hats, so they became my go-to. I purchased several, and each one gave me a tiny sense of control, style, and comfort. As we moved into winter in South Africa, warm woollen beanies became my best friends—practical and protective and easy to put on. Lifting my arms above my head for any length of time was a challenge.

Each piece of headgear became more than just something to cover up the baldness. It was armour. It was warmth. It was part of this journey

Erika and I met a lovely lady at the chemo unit on Monday. She was wearing the most beautiful headscarf. Naturally, we had to ask how she'd tied it so perfectly, and she kindly took the time to explain it all to us. It was a brightly coloured, ordinary scarf, but the way she wrapped it around her head and tied it made it an absolute masterpiece.

At that time, I couldn't quite lift my arms high enough or keep them up long enough to manage the scarftying myself. But I promised myself that one day soon—when my body was ready—I would give it a go. That little style tip gave me something fun to look forward to.

I was learning that bald can be bold *and* fashionable—especially with the right accessories.

My bra drawer was becoming my headgear drawer!

My precious Sam sitting in the surgeon's waiting room with me.

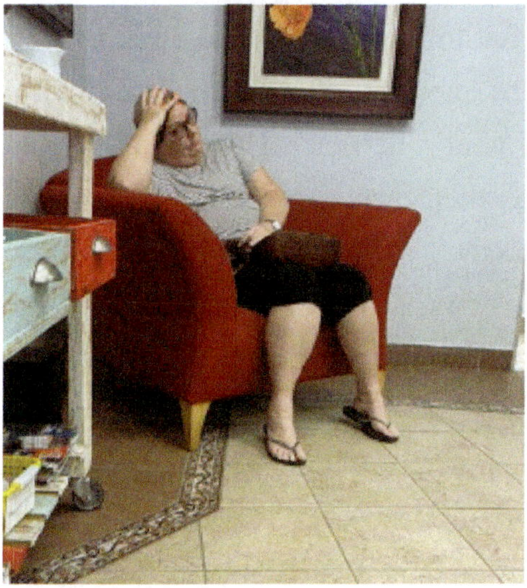

Me in the waiting room. You can see how tired I was!

8 April 2024
A Good Day

I was still adjusting to my body, my moods, and my emotions. And honestly, it's hard to put into words.

Some days, I felt like I could cry for hours. Other days, all I wanted was to jump in the car, head to a cozy coffee shop, and laugh with my sister, my daughter, and the rest of my precious family. The emotional shifts were unpredictable and out of my control. There were moments when even the idea of smiling felt impossible . . . and then, out of nowhere, a surge of energy would hit me, like I could climb Everest! (Let's be real—I'd probably make it fifty steps and then turn back. But hey, it's the thought that counts!)

Good news: I saw my surgeon, and all the stitches and staples were finally out. What a relief! I felt a little less tight. There was still one small area that hadn't healed completely, but the surgeon wasn't worried, so neither was I. He also gave me the go-ahead to restart my chemotherapy treatment plan. That was probably the best news! I immediately called the oncologist's offices and confirmed the appointment of 11 April.

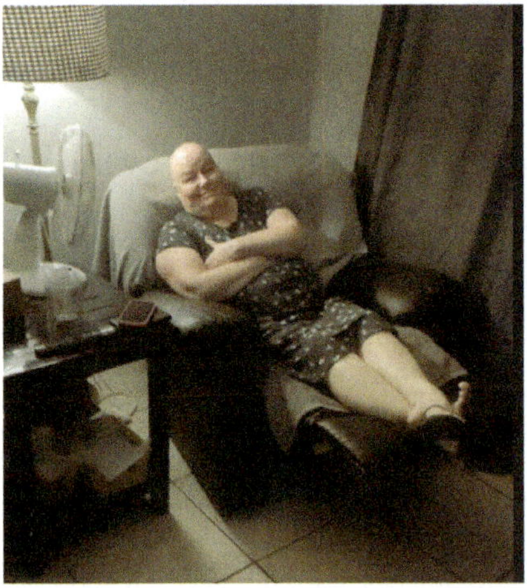

In my La-Z-Boy. I lived in this chair! It was a gift for my sixtieth birthday. Little did I know then how much I would need it four years later.

Looking quite good in a hat!

10 April 2024
Constant Curveballs and Turning a Corner

The past few months had been relentless. Life just kept throwing one curveball after another. It was the need for a mastectomy, then news that Erika was let go from her job as the company could no longer afford her services. Another curveball was the infections in my wounds. It just felt like everything that could go wrong did. Honestly, I had lost count. Some of these challenges were incredibly tough. My brother-in-law even joked that we must have a target on our backs . . . and I can't say I disagree!

However, amongst the curveballs, there was also good news! I'd qualified in South Africa as a financial planner a few years previously. Through word of mouth, a financial planner with a large company heard about me and offered me a position doing administrative work and reviews for him. It was a work-from-home position, which was absolutely perfect. It meant I could work whenever I had enough energy, even if it was in the middle of the night. It was basically for three days a week with a modest salary. But to me, it meant I had freedom and could cover my essential financial needs. I was beyond thankful.

11 April 2024
Chemo Number Two

My oncologist gave the green light to resume treatment, and it felt like another step forward. Today was chemo number two of the first four—and I was actually *grateful* to be back at it.

So far, apart from extreme fatigue, the side effects were manageable. I was blessed to avoid nausea this time around—something I did *not* take for granted. The only real visible sign? Bright-red cheeks from what's called "chemo flush." A strange little badge of honour, I guess.

When I saw my oncologist, I even asked if we could reduce the anti-nausea meds, hoping it might help me shed some of the chemo weight. He chuckled and told me that the cortisone was probably to blame—so he halved the dose. I crossed my fingers that it would help!

Chapter 7 – Back in the Fight

25 April 2024
This Is Breast Cancer in the Raw

I asked Erika to photograph me—to show what breast cancer *really* looks like—not the version you see in brochures or filtered Instagram posts. This is breast cancer, raw and real. I could see myself in the mirror, but seeing myself on "paper" was a real shocker.

I felt ugly.

I felt bold.

I felt fierce and strong.

I was angry. *Why me?*

I was determined to overcome.

I was going to beat this thing. And then I was

going to make myself attractive again! Yes, that was what I was going to do.

I was determined that this Big C would not get me under.

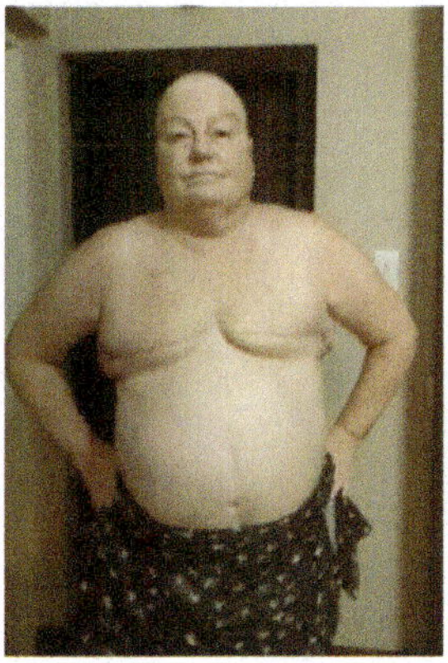

Just boobless and hairless me with huge cortisone belly! Wounds have healed well.

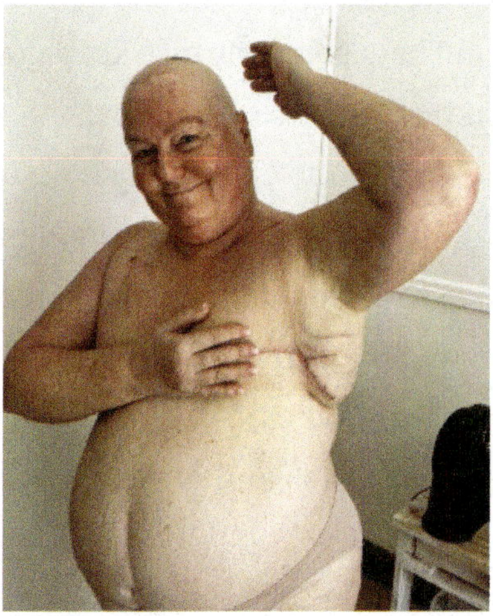

Massive cortisone belly.

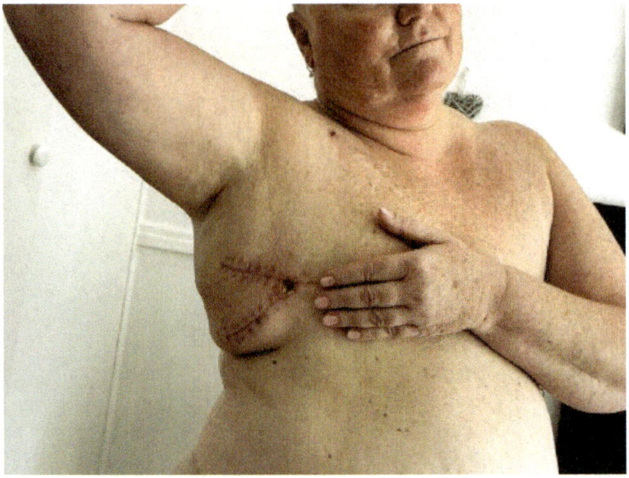

Ugly scars.

I share these photos in the hope that by being open and honest, by exposing the raw results of breast cancer, I might help someone else keep going. I might remind them that they are not alone.

Yes, you can see the chemo flush on my cheeks.

Yes, the cortisone belly is there, along with the flat chest, visible scars, and bald head.

But let me tell you something:

We are not our bodies.

Our souls, spirits, and inner beings—*that* is who we are.

The body? It's just the outer shell holding something much more precious inside. And whether we're sick or well, young or old, that outer shell will change.

So please . . . focus on the beauty of who you are within.

Be kind to yourself.

Be kind to others.

Because kindness doesn't leave scars—it leaves a lasting impression.

To all my fellow warriors out there: Keep fighting. Just fight on.

30 April 2024
Dreams

It was disorienting how quickly my feelings would change. Just a few days after taking those photos and feeling so calm and fierce, I found myself cringing at my reflection. Looking in the mirror was no longer a pleasure. Attempting to make myself look presentable was also no longer a pleasure. I just did the best I could with what I had. Sometimes, my arms were too tired to lift to tie a scarf around my bald head. I was glad for the turbans I'd found online that I could just pop on.

In fact, with my bald head, flat chest, and cortisone belly, you could have just sprayed me orange, and I would have been the Oros Man!

I dreamed of the things I wanted to do when I was better and had regained my strength. For the first time, I *really* wanted to get fit. I had always been a capable, strong woman. My difficult marriage had led me to learn to do everything myself. And I was able to do most things myself. As I aged, I sometimes asked my son-in-law for help. He and my daughter lived nearby while I was in South Africa. But most times, I did things for myself.

To suddenly be unable to even lift my arms above my head for any length of time was a real wake-up call. We take our bodies for granted when they are well and strong. And it's only when they are weak that we realise what a treasure a healthy body is.

I wanted to be fit enough to do the Amalfi walk in September 2025. (We paid for it nearly three years earlier in 2022, so I wanted to be well enough to do it.) I also wanted to hire a campervan and travel through Portugal, Spain, France, Belgium, Switzerland, Italy, Germany, and Austria. Maybe also Croatia, Bosnia, Hungary, and Slovakia. I would also love to visit Israel and go to all the places Jesus was. And then maybe one day, I'd go to Norway, Sweden, and Finland. And then, of course, I better consider finding my cottage in a village at the sea so I can retire sometime.

These dreams seem far-fetched, but they were the dreams that kept me fighting. The dreams that kept me from crumbling into a mental mess. The dreams that made me get up and work even when I felt awful and exhausted.

This was a chemo week, so it was me and the Red Devil again, plus all the other drugs they pumped into me. But I gladly and patiently accepted it because it would heal me. I was starting to get mouth sores, which are not nice. There was a wound from my mastectomy that was not healing. It looked awful and was quite uncomfortable and painful. It seemed that my immune system was not strong enough to heal the wound. So I decided to see what the next round of chemo held for me.

2 May 2024
My Ramblings, Giving to Charity, and Chemotherapy Number Three

I had been having pain on the left side of my back for a while. It wasn't all the time, but I occasionally needed to drink pain tablets. I mentioned it when I saw the oncologist today and had chemo. He examined me and said he didn't think it was anything to worry about, but he booked me for a CT scan on the day of my next chemo. So yes, those worry worms were crawling all over my mind and playing havoc with my thoughts and feelings and eating away at me! *What if the Big C has metastasised somewhere else?* I thought. *What if it has gone to my pancreas or liver? But then again,* I wondered, *what if it hasn't and it is just a normal ache from sitting too long in front of the laptop and working?* So the positive V was focussing on the normal ache and forgetting the ugly what-if.

My treatment plan consisted of four Red Devil chemotherapy treatments first, all 21 days apart. The last of them was planned for 23 May. The CT scan would be on the same day. Then I was not sure if I would have a break before I started the 12 weeks of weekly chemo (with a drug called paclitaxel) or if the oncologist would start the next phase immediately. I honestly couldn't complain about this chemotherapy. I wondered if the reason for minimal side effects was perhaps the drugs they gave me before giving me the chemotherapy, or if I was just lucky. Either way, I was incredibly thankful.

Yes, I had lost my hair. And yes, I was exhausted to the point of barely being able to walk or talk at times.

And yes, my tummy was sometimes uncomfortable. But that was really all I had experienced so far.

The administrative work I was doing was mundane, but I was thankful for the little bit it gave me. At least it paid my medical aid subscription, and I only worked a couple of hours. Erika started a BackaBuddy page for me to help with the mountain of medical bills not covered by medical aid. Someone asked me if the BackaBuddy was for reconstruction. I can assure you that it definitely wasn't for that. My oncologist would not even consider that for a long time. After the next chemo treatment ended, I needed to have four weeks of daily radiation. In fact, I was now an "old" woman. Who would care if I had boobs or not! And I hated a bra, so now I was happily braless!

Erika and I had also been actively collecting things for two charities: Caring Daisies (for people) and Wollies (for animals). We both felt that, as we were asking for help through BackaBuddy, it was important that we give as well. Asking for help isn't easy. It's humbling and feels vulnerable. But giving back helps ease the discomfort. It gave us a sense of balance and a sense of purpose. It might sound strange, but giving makes asking feel a little less heavy.

Being ill taught me a lot about need.

We all need something at some point in our lives, whether it is love, support, care, or even just a listening ear. There are so many vulnerable people and animals in the world that can't speak for themselves and can't ask. And that was hitting home for me more than ever because I'd been feeling that same helplessness. Cancer had forced me to rely on others, and that is not an easy space to be in.

Erika and I had put out word that we were collecting things—things we could either donate directly to the charities or sell to raise funds for them. People responded so generously. We spent time driving around to pick up bags and boxes from those who no longer needed certain things. Over time, we gathered enough to fill a small truck.

The plan was to deliver it all—one load to Caring Daisies and one load to Wollies.

Erika, with her incredibly generous heart, was also knitting blankets for children, cats, and dogs, pouring love into each of them one stitch at a time.

We took photos of our first delivery, and it was a moment of celebration and gratitude. So many wonderful people stepped in to help. And in doing so, they helped us heal too.

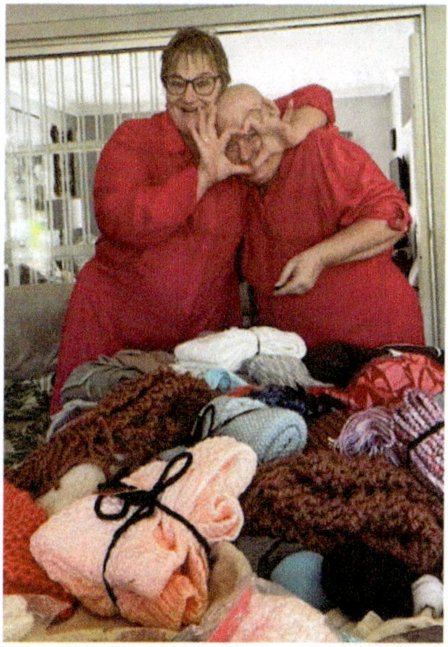

Erika and I doing our bit for charity.

10 May 2024
Complaining and Fatigue

I was experiencing a kind of fatigue—a tiredness and exhaustion I don't even have words for. It was unlike anything I had ever felt in my entire life.

Everything, even the smallest task, felt monumental. Brushing my teeth, getting dressed, walking to the kitchen—each one felt like climbing a hill with no summit in sight. The relentless tiredness didn't just affect my body. It was seeping into my emotions, leaving me fragile, tearful, and emotionally raw. And I hated that feeling.

It felt like it was stripping away all the positivity that I had tried to hold on to. I wished I had the right words to explain this sensation so it would make sense. But I couldn't quite capture it. It was just heavy in every possible way.

On top of this, my stomach seemed to have swollen even more, which only added to the discomfort. Moving, sitting, sleeping—everything felt harder. It was like my body had become unfamiliar and difficult to live in.

12 May 2024
My 65th Birthday

My precious daughter organised a wonderful birthday treat for me. We went to Wolwespruit, where we painted ceramics. I chose a heart-shaped plate and painted it with a sunflower, a cancer sign, and a message that holds huge meaning for me. I hoped I could look at this plate on my next birthday and be thankful for the journey and everything it taught me—but also very thankful that it was over. God willing!

My birthday treat. Thank you, my daughter and son-in-law.

When I thought of my future, I wondered, *Do I have a future? And if so, how long?* Of course, no one knows—not even those who do not have cancer! So I figured that perhaps it was one of those things I should not be concerned about. However, I assure you that if I am well by 2026, I will be hiring a campervan and travelling through Europe, starting in Portugal, for the whole of the summer.

21 May 2024
Netflix

I love watching limited series on Netflix. I'd recently started watching *From Scratch*—a delightful love story about two young people meeting and falling in love. As the series continues, they face different difficulties and challenges, as life would have it. And then, just as things seem to slowly be getting sorted out, *wham!* The Big Ugly C hits. The young man is diagnosed with a tumour in his knee.

Why am I telling you this? Well, I felt like I was sitting outside myself and looking in as I watched just how much the diagnosis affects first the man. He is told to have chemo first to shrink the tumour and then they will operate. You watch how he gets weaker and weaker and how he loses his hair. Then you watch as the wife becomes the caregiver, giving her all and feeling so much pain as she watches her husband suffer. You see how angry he gets because he knows she can't really understand. You see how tired and scared she gets because she is trying her best, and it doesn't seem good enough.

Eventually, he has the tumour removed, and the surgeon is happy to report that they got it all out. When the couple goes for his checkup, they are told that now the real chemo starts because, even though the tumour is out, the doctors don't know if a tiny bit of cancer decided to break free and run rampant through his body and perhaps attach to some organ and metastasise. You see the shock because they thought it was all over after the surgery.

But for me, it was mind-blowing to watch this happen to someone else and see how my thoughts and feelings were "normal" in a case like this. After a lumpectomy and double mastectomy, I still had to go through mounds of chemo that made me so ill and tired. You feel like you will never be normal again. I was thankful for my caregivers, but I knew they didn't really get it. It wasn't fair to expect them to get it regardless of how much they love me.

You see how a diagnosis like this affects every single aspect of your life, including work or business, family, finances, and emotions. There's just no area of life that is not affected by the cancer. It is like this huge storm cloud, dark and grey, that's hanging just above your head. You expect this cloud to break at any moment, sending a heavy deluge of pain, tears, and trauma raining down on you. But you do everything in your power to prevent this cloud from breaking. In fact, breaking isn't an option.

I am not sure if I am able to put into words how this series affected me. Just watching him put his head on his wife's shoulder and tell her that he is scared . . . I can't tell you how it tore my heart apart. I understood him. I knew.

Anyway, I don't mean to be negative. It was just mind-blowing to watch this and understand exactly what it is all about.

Sadly, at the end of the series, he passes away. It really brings the reality of cancer right up to your front door—pounding to come in and destroy everything within. It's a stark reminder of the battle so many of us are facing.

23 May 2024
Chemotherapy Number Four: The Last of the First Round

I saw my oncologist yesterday. We talked through the next phase: 12 weeks of weekly chemo. A *different* chemo. With a whole *new* set of side effects. The first thing he said was "This new chemo, called paclitaxel, will cause tremendous fatigue!"

I stared at him, thinking: *What? More tired than I already am? Seriously?*

"It will also cause pain in your lower back and legs," he continued. "Of the twelve treatments, the first four aren't too bad. The following four are worse, and the last four are really bad." This chemotherapy would also cause chemo rash, which is itchy and uncomfortable, as well as the chemo flush, which always left my face burning red.

Oh, the joy. (Insert eye roll and all the sarcasm I can muster.)

And just to top it off, he said, "You'll also likely have some neuropathy. Numb fingers. Numb toes." This is the kind of numbness that makes buttoning a shirt feel impossible. He said the symptoms *should* fade slowly after chemo ended.

It was like walking with wet sand in my shoes. Constantly.

It was awful.

I recently read another memoir of a woman who walked this cancer journey, and she speaks of neuropathy on the paclitaxel drug. She mentions that she was offered ice gloves and ice socks which decreased the possibility of severe neuropathy. As I read that, I was so unhappy that I didn't know about this while I was getting paclitaxel. It is now nearly a year later, and I still have neuropathy in my feet and on the very tips of my fingers. It could perhaps have been avoided if I used these special gloves and socks.

I think they work like the ice caps people put on their heads, to attempt to prevent hair loss during chemotherapy.

The next round of treatment, after the 12 rounds of chemotherapy, would be four weeks of daily radiation. So I was looking at another four months of treatments.

Then, hopefully . . . remission. Please, God.

I was tired. Really tired.

But I was also still here. Still showing up.

Still fighting.

On the day I received the last of the first four chemotherapy treatments, I was sent upstairs to the radiology department to have a CT scan. My oncologist just wanted to make sure that my back pain was not due to cancer of any kind. I was really thankful that he was thorough. I needed an "all-clear" CT scan.

I needed to first drink a liquorice-tasting drink: 250 ml every 15 minutes for an hour. I was then called into the room, and as per usual, I was given an IV so a dye could be inserted into my veins and course through my body so any abnormalities will be easily visible in the scan. It was over quickly, and I was released and free to go home and await the results..

Chapter 8 – Chemotherapy, Round 2

4 June 2024
Itchy Nipple!

Have you ever had an itchy nipple? I am sure you have. You can't really scratch your nipple, so I used to rub it between my thumb and forefinger to get relief from the itch. Most satisfying. Now, try that when your nonexistent nipple itches! The first time it happened, I automatically went to grab my nipple between my thumb and finger, and there was no nipple. But there definitely was an itch. It was frustrating. I can't put into words how it felt. It was just another reminder of what breast cancer women have to accept as the new normal.

11 June 2024
More Pain: Another Curveball!

And now, an ingrown toenail.

Not just annoying—badly infected.

The podiatrist had to remove a portion of the nail. Cue another incredibly painful injection—but enormous relief that the nail was gone. With chemo and diabetes, every wound I had was slow to heal, so I had to be extra cautious.

Looking at all of this in writing, I know it might sound like a list of complaints—but this is just the raw reality of cancer and its ripple effects. It's not all neat, tidy, and brave quotes. It's appointments, side effects, random dental dramas, and toenail infections that knock the wind out of you.

But despite everything, I was holding on to hope.

I *believed* this treatment would work. I was praying it would lead to remission and maybe—even just maybe—another 20 good years of life. God willing.

And after all this . . . I dreamed of the sea.

I wanted to spend a month or two by the ocean.

To walk along the shore. To breathe in the salty air. To listen to the waves. That's my healing place.

13 June 2024 First of 12 Weekly Chemotherapy Treatments, Good News, and Another Curveball

Good news first: The CT scan was all clear. My back ache was more than likely stress and muscle ache. I sighed a huge sigh of relief.

Chemo was officially underway again. I had lost two months! My second chemo should have been 11 March, but due to the mastectomy was started again on the 14 June. This was the first of 12 weekly treatments. Some days, I felt surprisingly okay and could actually get a few things done. Other days? Total fatigue. You just never know how you'll wake up feeling.

My body seemed to be having its own rebellion: I'd broken out in strange, raw red sores on my legs and arms. Thankfully, I had a psoriasis cream I'd found in Sedgefield that really helped soothe them.

I know that millions of people all over the world are diagnosed with some type of cancer every day. I also know that many are far worse than me, having stage 4 or worse. I also know that many cancer journeys are similar, with emotions ranging from disbelief to anger, and worry to acceptance—or something like that.

How can I explain the range of emotions, from far left on the spectrum to far right? Thoughts crowded my head, asking, *Why me?* I said to myself, *It's not fair* and *I am too young*. And then I felt fear, worry, and disbelief. And panic set in. All these feelings made my tummy flip every now and again.

And then on the far right of this feelings spectrum, I thought, *C'mon, V. Put on your big girl panties, as it's only stage 2 and grade 3. I've got this. It's no big deal.*

No one knew about these feelings or thoughts because they were all hidden deep inside me until they bubbled to the surface and erupted and I shouted at my sister (Sorry, Erika!) or burst into tears in a doctor's waiting room.

20 June 2024
Chemo Number 11

Instead of counting this as my second chemo appointment, I decided to do a countdown from 12. So this was chemo number 11. My daughter drove me to the hospital each week for my chemo treatments. She dropped me off at the oncology department, then headed up to the hospital's restaurant to grab breakfast and get some work done while I was having treatment. I am still beyond thankful for the love, support, and kindness she showed me every single day.

But I won't lie—walking from the oncology section to the restaurant was incredibly tough. It's just a short distance, but it's slightly uphill, and I was utterly exhausted by the time I reached it. I couldn't believe how weak my body had become. Each step felt like a mountain. Yet, even on the hardest days, I kept moving forward. I didn't have a choice but to keep pushing for my health and my family. This was a journey—sometimes a painfully slow one—but I was still here and still fighting. Plus, I was motivated to walk uphill from the chemo rooms to the restaurant because Sam had bought me an iced coffee and a chicken mayo sandwich! Yummy!

Through all the ups and downs, I came across something that really struck me—a statement from a cancer nurse who had worked with patients for over 30 years. She said, "Cancer ends either in remission or terminal. There is no other option."

That hit me hard. But as I reflected on it, it also sparked something inside me.

I *chose* remission.

I *chose* to fight.

I *chose* to believe in healing and stay as positive

as possible—even when the pain, fatigue, and curveballs kept coming.

Of course, I knew everything was ultimately in God's hands. But I also knew that He saw my heart and understood how deeply I longed for more life.

25 June 2024
A Question That Threw Me

Erika and I were standing in a queue at a supermarket to pay for our goodies when she suddenly asked me if I'd had any idea about what lay ahead when I was diagnosed with cancer. This question really made me think.

Honestly, I thought I would have the operation and some chemo, then be back in the UK by May or June at the latest and be working again. I never, in my wildest thoughts, imagined what I was going through.

Maybe it is just as well that I didn't know. It is easier to cope one day at a time than worry about the future. The weekly chemo was really, really not nice. After each session, I felt worse. I am unable to put the tiredness into words.

I was just trying my utmost to remain positive. There was really no other option. I had to believe that I would go into remission when all those treatments were over.

I was at my ugliest and hated looking in the mirror! But there was slight fluff on my head, so I was hopeful that my hair would grow back nice and thick. All of this was also teaching me that inner beauty is so much more important than outer. We just need to be patient and kind to others. To have integrity and honesty and be loving. I have many lessons to learn, and this was how God was preparing my soul for eternity.

I was also reminded of my precious father and his quiet strength and patience through his cancer journey. I was reminded how God put the finishing touches on his life and soul as he neared the end of his life's road.

27 June 2024
Chemo Number Ten

Thankfully, each treatment was happening every week, and we were slowly crawling towards the final chemotherapy day.

The day after chemo was always tough. The fatigue was unrelenting. It often took too much effort to even smile or speak. Most of the time, I was either in bed or sitting in my La-Z-Boy with my feet raised and my head back, taking several naps between watching TV.

I felt lazy, but I promise you that I was not. I simply didn't have the energy to do much else. Erika encouraged me to walk outside with our pets—we had five cats and two dogs—but I couldn't summon the energy to join her. I knew she didn't fully understand, and I didn't even realise sometimes how frustrated she had to be with my lethargy. I wished I could explain it better, but the words just didn't come.

It was a tough road, and while I'm incredibly grateful for the support, I still struggle to find the words to express everything I felt.

The nights were the worst. I couldn't sleep even after drinking a sleeping tablet. I tossed and turned for hours on end, going from one hot flush to the next. Every possible thought pushed its way into my already crowded mind, and I wanted to shout, "There is no more room for you! Just get out!" But the thoughts didn't listen.

I would open the curtain in my bedroom and stare up at the beautiful, quiet night sky. At one stage, the moon was so beautiful, and I ended up sharing some of my raging thoughts with the night sky and the moon, hoping I could get some answers or at least just hand them over to lessen the confusion within.

Talking to God and the universe did bring a sense of peace and quiet within. I would hear, "Just take a day at a time. You've got this!" And I then would slowly drift off to sleep.

4 July 2024
Chemotherapy Number Nine: The Quiet Acceptance of Treatment

I quietly accepted the chemo poison dripping into my veins through my port and watched as my fellow cancer patients received their treatments. We were all in different stages of our battles with different types of cancer.

After several chemotherapy treatments, I was now no longer a newbie. I watched the arrival of others who were clearly coming for the first time. I saw their fear and uncertainty, and I understood completely. My heart went out to them.

Cancer doesn't care who you are. It doesn't discriminate. It doesn't matter if you're male or female, rich or poor, educated or not, young or old, White or Black. Cancer doesn't care.

As I sat there looking across the large room, I saw that all the chairs were filled with men and women doing their best to accept their treatment, their fate, and their fight for wellness. I admired each one of them, and I drew strength from their presence and courage.

I also watched their caregivers. It is so important to have loving, unconditional care and support while travelling this road called cancer. You cannot do it alone. No one can. It isn't just the physical aspect. Cancer affects every aspect of life: financial, spiritual, emotional, and physical. It also impacts relationships and careers. It touches just everything, and it is daunting, scary, and overwhelming.

Most of the caregivers I observed were family or close friends. We must never underestimate how cancer affects a caregiver. I honestly had no idea until well after my treatment was done.

Our caregivers love us, so they want to fix us. But they can't.

They want us to get better in their time, but we can't.

They don't want to see us battle and struggle, but they are helpless.

So it leads to depression and burnout for many caregivers.

If you are a caregiver, take a break. You need it, as does the cancer sufferer.

My tummy had started playing up. I often didn't make it to the loo in time! What a mess. And how embarrassing. I now had to plan when I ate because I couldn't leave the house if I had eaten. My tummy could suddenly need to empty itself, and there was no warning.

For my son-in-law's birthday, I ordered a special cake. And we planned a braai (barbecue) for Sunday. I hoped I would feel strong enough to join the party.

As the chemotherapy continued, my tummy was still behaving so badly, and I was often caught unawares. I was even considering purchasing pull-ups, but it wasn't like having a leaking bladder. A colon that can't be controlled leaves a mess and a smell. Oh, it was really awful. I felt like I should just remain housebound.

You know, my tummy sometimes needed to go, and I couldn't make it running from the lounge to the bathroom. That was how fast it would go. I didn't share this with many because I felt so embarrassed.

25 July 2024
Chemotherapy Number Six: Halfway!

Ha, I have reached halfway. Only six more treatments!

The side effects were really kicking in. I was getting numb fingers and toes. I had continued fatigue and the unpredictable tummy. I developed sores on my legs, which I mentioned before. When I asked another oncologist about the sores, she told me that they were caused by the cancer drug I was receiving.

It works a lot like Efudix, which is a strong topical medicated cream that destroys abnormal cells that make up the solar keratoses on your skin. About three years previously, I was prescribed Efudix for my face. It caused sores where there were abnormal cells on my face. But as the sores healed, all those precancerous sun spots were gone. My legs were covered in sun spots. I loved the sun when I was young and spent hours and hours at the beach. Now I was paying the price.

While I mention this, I may as well tell you that I also had a basal cell carcinoma removed from just above my upper lip about three years before my breast cancer diagnosis.

1 August 2024
Chemotherapy Number Five

Erika and Pieter organised a weekend away for us. It was a lovely long weekend at a resort not far out of Pretoria. I spent lots of time in the warm outdoor pool. It was a cold winter in South Africa, so this was amazing. Warm water is so relaxing. And I was still drinking my ice-cold water and eating my ice.

Oh, I haven't told you about the ice eating! It is so frustrating to those around me because it makes a noise, but I am constantly craving ice. I looked it up. Apparently, it is a symptom of iron deficiency. That is my excuse, and I am sticking to it. I go through bags of ice a week.

8 August 2024
Chemotherapy Number Four, Postponed

When I arrived at the oncology unit for my chemotherapy, I was told that the oncologist had decided not to give me chemo, as my red blood cell count was way too low and my body too weak. Another delay! I could feel it in how absolutely exhausted I was. I was disappointed because the delay just extended the end of the treatment. But at the same time, I was thankful because I was exhausted. There are no words to describe this kind of exhaustion.

My iron, which should have been between 50 and 120, was 484. That also made me feel quite unwell. It was strange to think that this was all caused by the chemo—the very thing that was trying to heal me

15 August 2024
Chemotherapy Number Four, Hopefully!

The next week had come, and I was having my chemo. I was so excited because the chemo number three, two, one countdown was in sight! After today, there was only chemo three, then two, then one—and then done!

The neuropathy was at its worst. I had numbness and tingling in my feet and hands. It felt like burning, stabbing, or shooting pains. It also caused a loss of balance and coordination and definitely muscle weakness, especially in my feet. I felt useless and certainly hoped I would get my strength back.

22 August 2024
Chemotherapy Number Three

I was still so excited, as the end of chemo was in sight!

I arrived at the oncology department, and again my blood counts were not good. I told them about the neuropathy, so they adjusted my dose. But fortunately, they still gave me the chemo. I honestly dreaded a further extension.

My nonexistent left boob had developed another seroma. If it got bigger, they would send me to the radiologists to drain it. This caused some panic because I wondered if they would find cancer cells floating in the seroma. Fortunately, the seroma did not get any bigger, so they didn't draw any fluid.

When I came home after chemo, I found myself sitting in my La-Z-Boy with so much nerve pain in my fingers and feet. All my muscles were aching. My blood sugar reading reached coma-stage heights at 29.4, so I had to take an insulin injection. I felt absolutely, awfully ill.

By the way, on the evening of every day that I had chemotherapy, my blood sugar climbed to around 30. So I was taking insulin injections to help control it. Erika was so sweet. She checked up on me during the night to make sure I was okay. I appreciated that more than she knows.

My oncologist prescribed Nurika and Neurobion today for the neuropathy, and I was waiting for delivery from the pharmacist and hoping it would help with the pain in my feet and hands.

And you know the strangest thing that happened? I had been wearing specs for about 25 years because I could not see far. I had multifocal specs for seeing far distance and seeing at a computer distance. And there was a tiny section for reading. But I had never needed specs to read. Well, it was flipped completely. I didn't need specs for distance at all, but I could not read without magnifying glasses (which I bought out of desperation). I couldn't see anything on my phone without these magnifiers. How weird is that? The oncologist told me to wait about four weeks after chemo stopped before I had my eyes tested. Maybe it would flip back again. Who knows.

Through those 12 weeks of treatment, it was just a case of putting my head down, accepting the many side effects, and looking forward to the end. Sounds simple enough . . . but it truly wasn't.

5 September 2024
Final Chemotherapy Treatment

The day of my final chemotherapy treatment had arrived, and it was at eight a.m. Nice and early so I could celebrate afterwards. Mmmmm . . . what a joke. There was no energy for celebration. Only a deep thankfulness in my heart that I'd made it that far. The nurses were absolute darlings at this oncology unit, and I got a lovely photo of them all surrounding me. I also got advice about the radiation and how to look after my skin. I soaked up all the advice and love. It made me feel positive, hopeful, and alive.

I looked awful, though. Bald head, huge tummy, and flat chest. Where has Verena gone?

The amazing nurses that cared for me during all those weeks of chemo. They just need wings!!

Chapter 9 – Radiation

9 September 2024
Appointment with Radiation Oncologist

I had my appointment with the radiation oncologist to discuss the next phase of treatment: radiation. After reviewing all my medical records, she informed me that I'd need 30 radiation sessions—every weekday for six weeks. I was shocked. I'd originally been told I'd need only four weeks of daily radiation. Now it was going to be six weeks, and I would have to adjust my focus again.

I have learned that expectation leads to disappointment. Here again was a prime example. I expected four more weeks of treatment, only to be told it would be six. When will I learn not to expect things? The disappointment is always intense.

Cancer radiation is different to chemotherapy. The radiation uses high-energy radiation to kill cancer cells and shrink tumours. It works by damaging the cancer cells' DNA and therefore preventing them from growing and dividing. This means that radiation is directed at the area surrounding where the cancer was found. So it destroys cancer cells in a specific location. Chemotherapy drugs, on the other hand, go throughout the body to kill or slow the growth of cancer cells.

The first 25 radiation sessions were mapped out to target my body from the middle of my chest towards the left and end at the right side of my back. It would stretch from just below my chin to above my waist.

The final five sessions would be "targeted radiation" focused specifically on my left chest scar only. Apparently, that's a common site where cancer can return. At this point, my reaction was simply "Whatever. Just do what you must. Let's get this done."

The doctor explained that once the radiation team finalized the strength and details of my treatment, I'd have to go in for a marking session. They'd mark my body to ensure that each radiation session was precisely aligned, targeting only the areas that needed it.

Another chapter of my cancer journey had begun. I would take it one day at a time, just as I had until now.

12 September 2024
Another Bump in the Road: Sinus Trouble and Dental Drama

It seemed that having to deal with cancer and the treatment was not enough. Fate, my body, or the universe had decided that I needed more physical challenges—physical challenges that were exponentially worse because of a very weakened immune system thanks to the cancer treatment. I felt like a hamster on a wheel just going round and round. One thing led to that, which led to the next thing, and so on!

Did I tell you I had root canal treatment sometime back? Well, it turned out that the dentist pierced my sinuses during the procedure. For months, I'd had unexplained nosebleeds and constant discomfort. Recently, my face had swollen on the right-hand side—it was red, painful, and just awful.

I saw another dentist today, and he confirmed that my sinuses had been pierced. I now had a large ulcer in that area. So yes—more antibiotics, more healing, and more patience required. My body was taking one knock after the other.

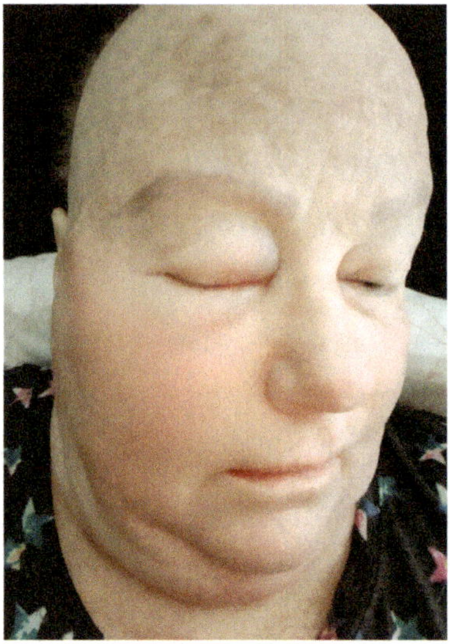

Swollen face from an infected abscess and ulcer. Could I get any uglier?

16 September 2024 One Thing Done and Another Unexpected Twist

Today started off pretty normal. I went to see my podiatrist for a checkup on my toes. Good news: They were healing well, and she said I no longer needed to come back. One more medical thing ticked off the list. What a relief!

But while I was sitting in the chair, I suddenly started feeling very ill. A sharp, awful pain in my chest hit me, and I was struggling to breathe. For a moment, I honestly thought I was having a panic attack. My podiatrist could see something was wrong just by looking at me. Thankfully, I was in a medical facility, and they quickly got me into a wheelchair and took me straight to a doctor.

Within minutes, I was on a drip and being treated. The doctor diagnosed a severe gastritis attack. Let me tell you, that pain was no joke. Another side effect of the cancer treatment and a severely weakened immune system. Thankfully, with the right medication, the pain eased within the hour, and I started to feel better.

As always, my darling daughter came to fetch me and take me home. She'd been my rock through all of this, and I am still endlessly grateful.

I am still standing. (Just a little more bent over today!)

27 September 2024
Radiation Prep: Measured, Marked, and Slightly Panicked

The day of my visit to the radiation centre arrived. I was there to be measured and tattooed for the upcoming radiation treatments. I'll be honest—it wasn't the greatest experience.

They had to measure me very precisely, and part of the process involved holding my breath for at least 30 seconds. When you do that, they actually cut off your oxygen for that time. Yes, there's a little device in your hand that you can squeeze if you need to breathe again, but still—it's unsettling. The first few times brought on near panic, but I eventually managed to relax and got better at it.

I recently read a book written by a cancer survivor in Australia. When she described her experience with radiation, she mentioned the "breath hold" technique. The nurses had explained to her that because the radiation was being targeted on the left side, close to the heart, holding a deep breath helps reduce the radiation dose to the heart.

I'm so glad I came across this, because I never actually knew why I had to hold my breath during my own treatment—and, silly me, I never thought to ask!

Reading this made me realise just how valuable other people's cancer memoirs can be. They truly help fill in the gaps and make you feel less alone.

And here's where I had to smile: The three tiny dots immediately reminded me of that *Friends* episode where Phoebe and Rachel get tattoos. Phoebe was too scared and got only a single small dot. She says it's how her mother sees her from Heaven. At least I found the humour in the situation. And sometimes, that's what keeps us going.

1 October 2024
Just Another Medication . . .

The specialists had to add another medication to the mix—this time to help with the lingering side effects of chemo. Chemotherapy drugs differ; therefore, their side effects differ. However, the side effects can last for several months or even years, with some lasting a lifetime. Side effects—such as fatigue, nerve damage, neuropathy, and even hearing loss—can linger or even be permanent. But you know what? You accept those side effects because the alternative is too scary to think about.

I had been prescribed four weekly Exprex injections, which stimulate the bone marrow to produce more red blood cells. It's typically used to treat anaemia in adults undergoing chemotherapy for solid tumours, malignant lymphoma, or multiple myeloma, especially when there's a need for a blood transfusion.

This had been prescribed back on 8 August, the same day they postponed my chemo because my red blood cell count was too low. I received authorisation from my medical aid for it only now—nearly two months later! But better late than never, right?

So now, I'd added weekly self-injections to my routine. One more step towards healing. One more task on the journey. And I'd keep ticking them off, one by one.

9 October 2024
First Radiation

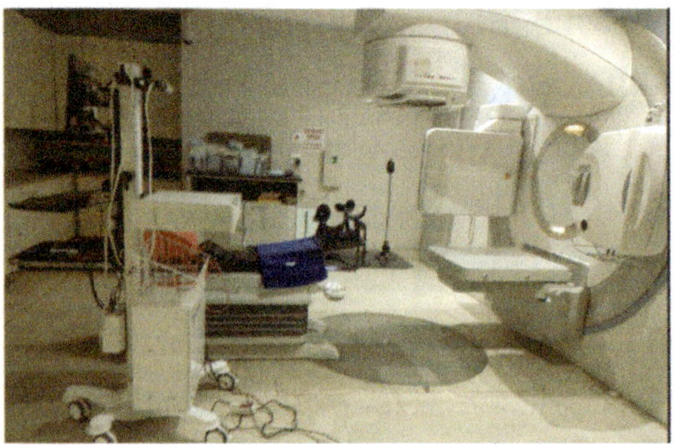

Radiation machine.

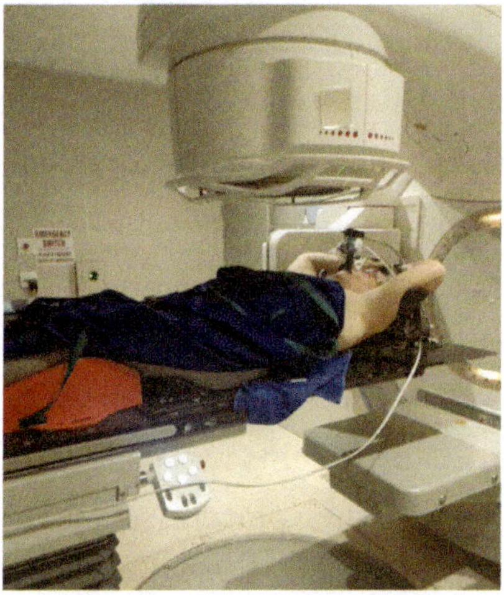

Being prepped for radiation.

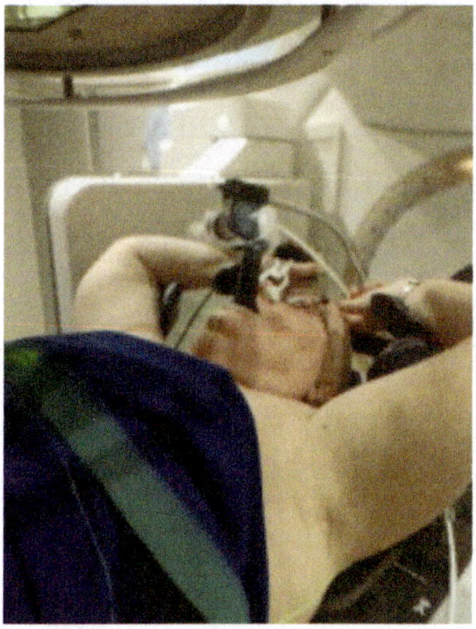

They block your nose and put a tube in your mouth so you cannot breathe when the radiation is applied. That took some getting used to.

My final round of treatment started on 9 October. I arrived at the radiation department, and a nurse came to see me and explain how things would work. I was given my own breathing apparatus and a gown, which was stored in a box with my name and would be mine till I finished radiation. I changed into the gown and waited to be called into the radiation room. Just looking at the machine was quite terrifying, but I also knew it had healing powers, so I quietly accepted my fate. The nurses were so lovely and kind, and they explained things to me. I wanted a photograph of myself on the radiation machine, and they kindly took a picture for me. They then adjusted the machine, moving me up and down and right and left until I was in the exact position I had to be in so the radiation would be directed exactly at the targeted area as prescribed.

The machine made a kind of beep when the radiation was being applied. During that time, I had to hold my breath. I was so nervous, but I seemed to manage.

As the days passed and I started getting used to the routine and the beeps, I knew that there were three beeps of radiation first. Then the machine moved towards my back, and there were two beeps. It moved again to the top, and there were three beeps. Then towards the right and three more beeps. And then all done.

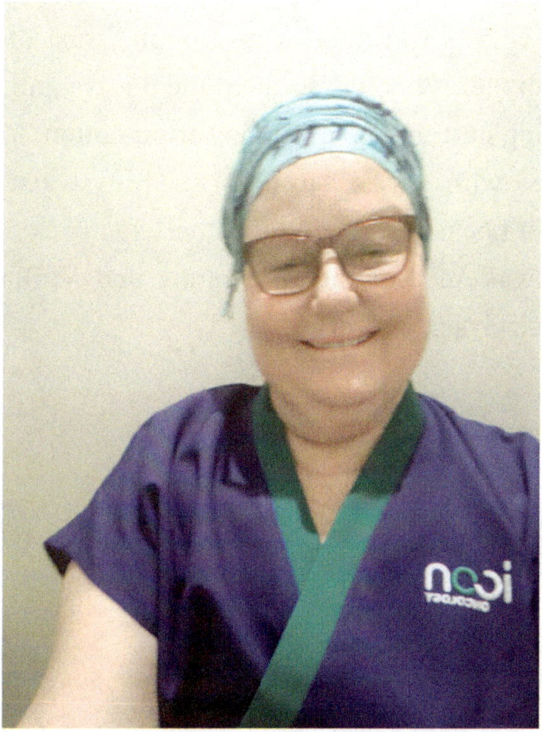

Waiting to be called in for radiation.

I was at the radiation centre every day. After three weeks, my skin was starting to burn. And each day, it got worse and worse. It was bleeding and hot and itchy and scabby. I had tried umpteen different creams, sprays, and lotions. Sam came to me every evening before bed and lathered my back. She was such a caring, loving daughter.

I can't express just how painful the radiation burns became. My skin was tight and painful. The weather was warming up as South Africa headed for summer. This did not help the burns at all. Any clothing hurt them—even the softest cotton. I often walked with only a sarong around my waist, as I couldn't bear clothing on my chest and back.

It was embarrassing, frustrating, and debilitating. Oh, the joys of cancer!

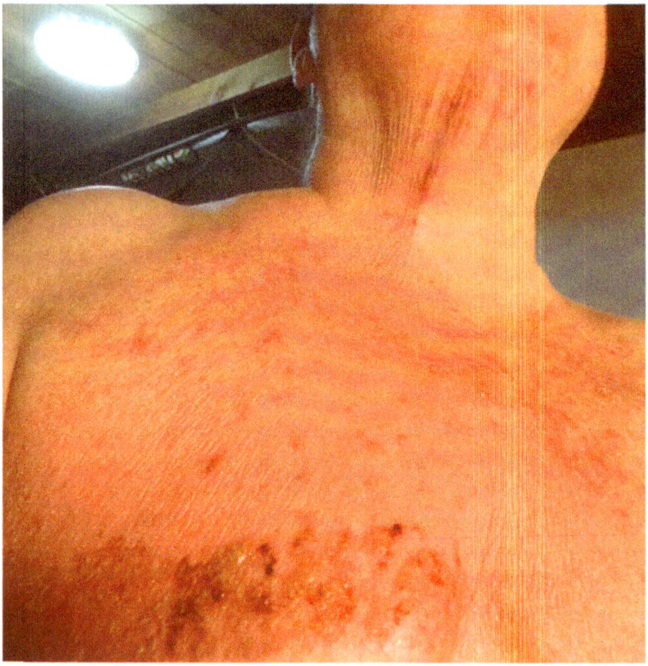

Radiation burns. So painful. Raw, blistering, and bleeding.

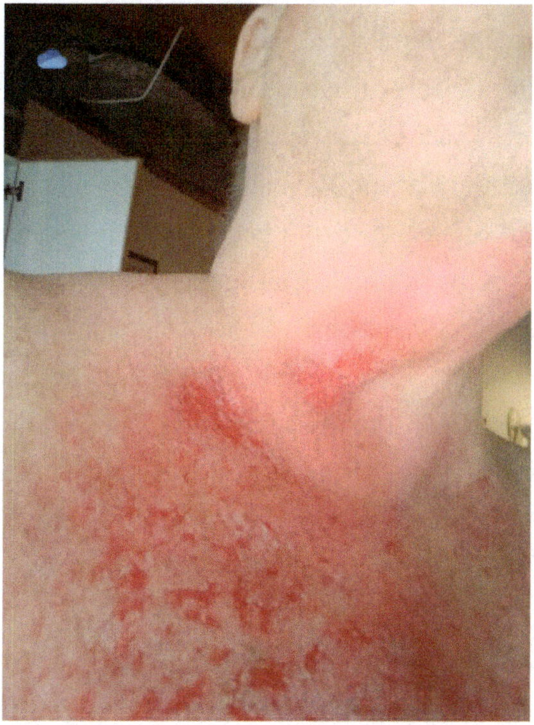

So painful.

26 October 2024
One Year Since Diagnosis

On 26 October 2024, I "celebrated" (wrong word altogether) a year since I'd heard these words: "Sorry to have to tell you, but you have breast cancer." Little did I know then what lay ahead. Perhaps it was just as well that God veils the future from our sight! I couldn't believe it had been a year. Nor could I believe how sick I really was during chemo.

As I think back, I am so sorry for Erika and Pieter—but especially Erika because we are sisters and she loves me so much. Caregivers suffer just as much as the one with cancer!

I was a walking zombie from the beginning of the year. I didn't really see myself, but I know Erika saw my face every day. And it was a miserable, half-asleep face with droopy eyes and no smile. I know this depressed her. I see this now in hindsight. I know I could not help it, but I am sorry.

For the time being, I was just hanging in there. Although the side effects of radiation were way less than chemo side effects, I still had the neuropathy in my feet and hands, which was really uncomfortable. It felt like having wet sand in my shoes. My calf, arm, and shoulder muscle pain was quite bad. I lived on painkillers for that. I was a wee bit tired. But those were all side effects from radiation.

17 November 2024
End Is in Sight

I had only three radiation treatments left, so *wooo-hooo* was appropriate! Except that I had the most awful radiation burns. I can't begin to tell you how painful, itchy, and uncomfortable they were. My skin felt like leather, and it felt nothing like sunburn! They tell you it will be like sunburn. Urgh, no! They lie!

My chest up to my neck and to under my arm was burned. My back on the left side was burned. The creams and sprays might help for about two minutes and then it burned again.

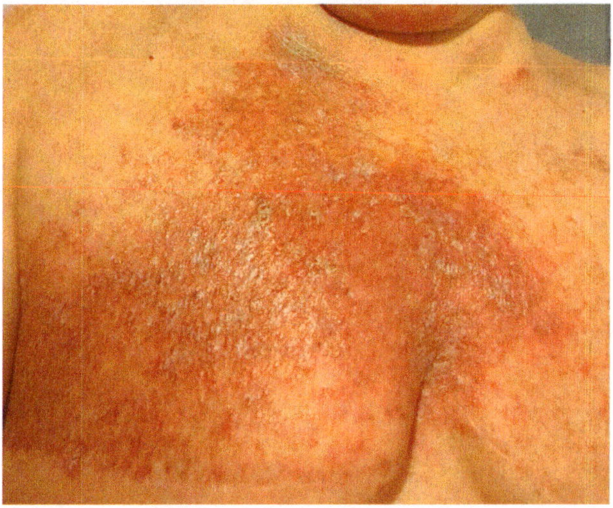

It's hard to explain the pain this caused. And it went all the way to the middle of my back.

My precious daughter came faithfully every night to apply lotion to my back. I also had a fan blowing on me all night. Now that summer was coming, it was getting super hot in Pretoria again.

I was so, so sore! I was sitting there with a sarong over my shoulders because clothing hurt.

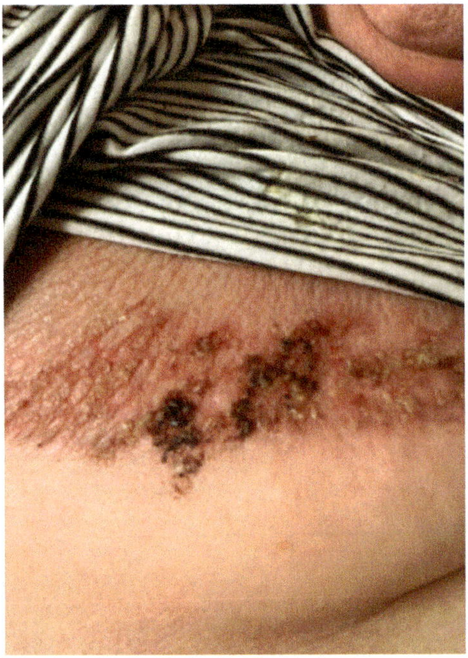

I had to have five extra radiations directly on the wound of the left breast. Apparently, cancer cells like to target that area!

Patience was the word of the day!

19 November 2024
Final Radiation

My first radiation started on 9 October. I had 30 radiation treatments, and they were every day, Monday to Friday. Now, the day of my final radiation session had arrived.

And I rang the bell! The kind nurses took photos and a video. And then they said, "We hope to never see you again." Yes, my sentiments exactly!

Ringing the bell because all the radiation sessions were complete! Look at the joy!

I was due to see the surgeon on 27 November with regard to the huge lumps under my arms. I was hoping he would be able to do something about them. Then I was going to see the oncologist on 2 December. I hoped to find out I was cancer-free. *That* would be a true celebration!

My hair was growing, but a hairdresser advised that I keep it shaved for a while because then it would come back thicker. So I was following her advice for the time being.

This illness taught me to not plan anything far into the future; however, I was hoping to visit my son Richard in Cape Cod, USA, in mid-December and stay with him till early February. Then I would fly directly to London so I could start working again. It was winter in Cape Cod, and I hoped for snow. Richard lived within walking distance of the sea! I couldn't wait to dress warmly and walk on the beach with the wind in my nonexistent hair, the sea sound in my ears, and the sea salt smells in my nose!

Chapter 10 – Waiting

25 November 2024
Appointment with Radiation Oncologist

The doctor was very concerned about the burns. They were red and raw and bleeding in places. I had tried every kind of cream and lotion you can imagine. So many people gave advice, but honestly, nothing really helped. Some of the applications cooled the skin for a short while, but then it started burning again. I battled to wear any tops because it hurt so much.

I was staying with Sam at the time. My poor son-in-law was exposed to his mother-in-law walking around topless because she was really battling to cover the burns! But hey! I had no boobs, so why couldn't I walk topless? That was my argument, and I stuck to it. Nic, my son-in-law, was amazing.

He also helped me so much. I am beyond thankful to them both.

27 November 2024
Breast Surgeon Appointment

Today, I saw the surgeon who did my mastectomy. I wanted to know about these huge lumps under my arms and whether he could remove them. He told me that a plastic surgeon had to do it and that he couldn't assist me any further. So much for that appointment! It cost me R900, and I had no resolution. Sometimes, the medical profession disappoints.

But I was about to find out just how badly medical professionals can disappoint!

2 December 2024
Appointment with My Oncologist

This was the day I had been hoping for! It was the day I was going to see my oncologist after all the treatments, and he, hopefully, would tell me I was in remission. I had had a lumpectomy, axillary dissection, double mastectomy, 16 chemotherapy sessions, and 30 radiation blasts. My expectation was to hear that I was cancer-free.

I woke that morning feeling a little anxious but also really relieved that 13 months of ups and downs might be coming to an end.

I felt like I was standing right on the top of this mountain I had been climbing, and it was almost time to exhale.

I arrived at the oncologist rooms early and was greeted with lots of smiles from the staff. They really were a friendly bunch—just what cancer patients need.

I was called in to see the man who, 11 months earlier, had drawn me a diagram outlining my treatment. I had a lot of faith in him, and now I was hoping for the all clear. He examined me and said he thought I was fine. He suggested that the port stay in, as we might need it again sometime in the future! *What does that mean?* I wondered.

He then sent me for blood tests and a CT scan right after seeing him.

So off I went to the pathologist's office first. These nurses were amazing. I couldn't believe how they found a vein in an arm that does not give up its veins easily! And normally, I didn't feel a thing. Wonderful! The little kindnesses and quiet talents of people like them always stick with me.

Then it was time to head upstairs to the ultrasound/ scan department. I had to drink 1 L of liquorice-flavoured liquid (as per before)—250 ml every 15 minutes. Then the contrast scan would be done.

And that was me done for the day. My oncologist told me that he would contact me the next day with the results and to confirm that I was in remission.

3 December 2024
Waiting for That Call!

I was anxious all day as I waited for my phone to ring. I was waiting to hear the oncologist's voice say, "You are in remission"—quite the opposite of what I'd heard 13 months earlier when he said, "I am sorry to tell you that you have cancer."

But the phone didn't ring. Eventually, late in the afternoon, I called the surgery, only to be informed that the oncologist had already gone home and would speak to me the next day.

Oh, I wonder if doctors realise what that does to a patient. Anger, anxiety, disappointment . . . all negative emotions rush in and just cause further inward turmoil.

4 December 2024 Would I Hear Today I Am in Remission?

Today, I thought. *Yes, today he must call me and tell me. Today.*

I waited. I waited. I waited.

Eventually, late in the morning, I called his rooms. His secretary advised me that he had received the results and she would email them to me.

She emailed me the CT scan report as well as the blood test results. I was a bit dumbfounded. *Is the doctor not going to speak to me and explain the reports and results?* I wondered. I didn't understand. Was I in remission or was I not?

I emailed her back with questions—specifically whether I was officially in remission—and asked her when the doctor would speak to me.

Would you believe me if I said that his secretary emailed me back with answers to my questions but without saying whether I was officially in remission or not?

In fact, the CT report stated that there was a lymph node that was larger than it should be. I quote: "Few sub centimetre lymph nodes noted right pretracheal and precranial regions. Right subcarinal lymph node

17 x 9mm, requires follow-up. Malignant infiltration of normal sinus hilar lymph nodes not excluded."

As per good ol' Google: "In the subcarinal region, 1.5 cm is usually considered to be the upper limit of normal."

My oncologist never spoke to me again, even after several emails and phone calls. All I got from his surgery was a message from the secretary to say that things were stable at the moment. That was the message from the oncologist. He had nothing further to add. He would send the reports to my oncologists in England, and they would assist me further.

I can't tell you how distressing this was for me. I had this swollen lump in my neck, and I didn't know what it was. Perhaps it was nothing to worry about. But let me tell you, when you have had cancer and have gone through rough treatments, learned about cancer, and read many memoirs by cancer patients, any lump or strange symptom is enough to cause panic in your chest!

I felt a bit like a deflated balloon. Everyone said I mustn't worry—that I was free of cancer—and that the doctor would have called me if there was something to worry about. I agreed, but he also said the port must stay in just in case I needed chemo in the future. So please forgive me if I felt anxious!

Anyway, I was fortunate to get an appointment with my GP in the UK. I was going to arrive there on 30 January 2025 at seven a.m. and would be seeing him at six p.m. I would give him all the reports I had. I still didn't have the report from the oncologist stating how much and what chemo I had received or how much or what radiation I was given. Clearly, the doctors in the UK would need that information. I decided that I would keep emailing him and hopefully get it before 30 January.

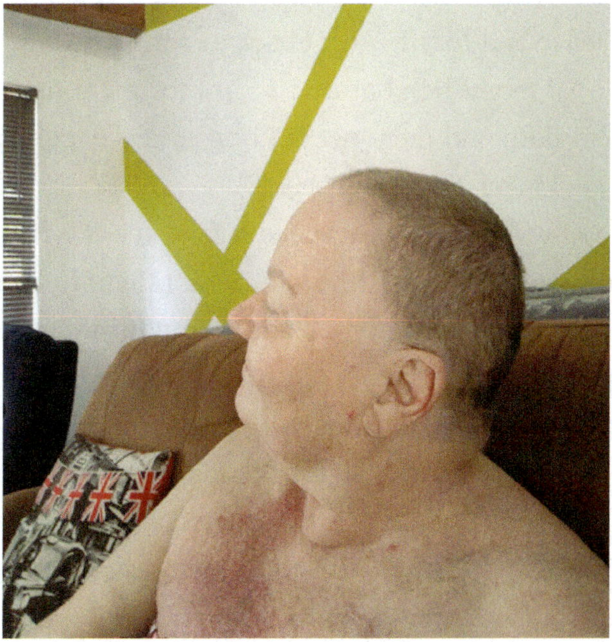

Some good news: my hair was growing.

24 December 2024
Flying to Cape Cod

It had been a year since we'd celebrated Erika's sixtieth birthday. I couldn't believe how fast time had gone and what we'd all experienced in 2024—a year filled with drama, pain, joy, laughter, love, hope, and family.

It was time to say goodbye to my wonderful family, without whom I would not have managed. Sam and Nic took me to the airport. I knew it was time to leave and for life to get back to normal (whatever normal might be), but it was hard for me. I hugged them both and then just held on to my daughter a while longer. She is my heart.

I flew to Boston to spend a few weeks with my darling son Richard. I had a pleasant flight to Heathrow, where I had a layover, and then to Boston. It was just wonderful to walk out of the terminal and see my beautiful son waiting with open arms. Oh, I am blessed with the wonderful children I have.

The travelling was extremely exhausting. Lifting my heavy suitcases off the baggage carousel took superhuman, mind-over-matter powers. Thankfully, my strong son took over.

It was extremely cold there, which was great when the hot flush hit. I just had to pop my head outside, and I cooled off instantaneously.

25 December 2024 Christmas Day

My son and I spent a quiet and peaceful day enjoying the snow. I love it when snow is falling. The quietness and the white cover all imperfections till you eventually just have this pristine, clean landscape. It is so bright that you need sunglasses, and all is still.

I spent the next few weeks resting and sleeping—a lot! I got books from the library and read—a lot! All cancer books.

Neuropathy was still an ongoing problem. I had my last head shave before I left South Africa, so now I was leaving my hair to grow. My son gave me rosemary oil and vitamin E oil, which I mixed and rubbed into my scalp. Apparently, it helps the hair grow and get thicker.

I was being put on tamoxifen for five years and was waiting to receive a follow-up regimen once I was back in the UK.

I'd also started experiencing brain fog—just another drug-related side effect to add to the mix. Tamoxifen causes serious memory problems. I had read about many women who were on it after breast cancer and then went off it because the brain fog affected their high-powered jobs. Fortunately, I am only a carer, so I don't really need much of a brain or a good memory!

Now my focus is my health – intermittent fasting, keto and walking/exercise. I need to get ready for my trip to Italy in September 2025 with Irene. We are doing a five-day walking holiday along the Amalfi Coast. (I hope nothing prevents it next year!)

26 December 2024–28 December 2024 Days of Rest and Rejuvenation

I needed these days of rest, away from everything and everyone, more than I'd realised. It was just my son and me, and he was often busy. We sometimes caught the bus and went to a nearby village for lunch or did some shopping. Sometimes, I walked to the library and sat there for a while. But that was all. I was enjoying the cold. I loved dressing warmly in leggings, boots, beanies, gloves, scarves, and jackets when we went out. Inside, it was toasty warm.

I don't want to bore you . . . I just want to remind you that your health is your wealth, so take care of it. And remember, cancer does not discriminate. Ladies, go for your mammograms. People, don't ignore suspicious symptoms. Remember that it is *your* body and not the doctors'. You need to take control away from the specialists who think they are gods and make them listen to you. I have read so many books about cancer patients who were dismissed by doctors as hypochondriac or melodramatic. Yet all that time, they'd had cancer, which had metastasised and spread by the time it was diagnosed. It makes me furious!

Let me stop before my fury burns up the page!

29 December 2024
What Cancer Would You Choose?

A dear friend was recently diagnosed with ovarian cancer, and it knocked me for a six! I don't know how to say this, so I am just going to say it as it comes . . . If you had to get cancer but could choose the type of cancer, what would you choose? Have you ever thought of that? I have read two memoirs by women with breast cancer and two memoirs by women with ovarian cancer. I have also read hundreds of snippets by other cancer patients with all different sorts of cancer—lung, throat, pancreatic, and liver. My own precious father had tongue cancer.

So I ask again: If you had to get cancer, what type would you choose? I know it is an impossible question, as well as rhetorical. It is just that thoughts, questions, and scenarios are running riot in my head!

We all have to die. We know that. But I guess we don't face it head-on because death is somewhere far in the distance. We can ignore it as if it doesn't exist. You know those movies where people are driving on a long, lonely road and it is hot? The view is hazy from the heat and dust, and they just keep driving to reach some destination . . . kinda far, far in the distance. It's something like that.

But then you get a diagnosis that brings death right up to your front door. It is in your face, and you have no idea how to react. But instinct kicks in, and you start to do all you can to fight. To live. I wonder why. I believe completely and without a doubt that there is a Heaven. I believe it is a wonderful place where there will be no more tears or fears. So why fight to live and not welcome Heaven? For me, the simple explanation is that I know this life. I don't know the hereafter. So I fight for the familiarity of life as I know it.

And then it takes me back to my question: If I had to get cancer, which cancer would I choose if I had a choice?

I honestly don't know.

These thoughts tumble out of my head through my fingers and onto the keyboard before I can stop them. I can't make sense of them.

The one thing I do know is that when you have cancer, you definitely have a BC and an AC, and that will live with you for the rest of your life. BC: Before Cancer. AC: After Cancer. And AC will never be the same as BC was.

I was reading something that someone said. (I have brain fog or, as they call it, chemo fog, which stays with you long after chemo finishes. So please pardon that I can't remember who wrote this.) Anyway, they said you can lose everything in life and still recover. But once you lose your health, you have lost the best of you. It is best, therefore, to attempt to stay healthy—eat well, move more, choose happiness, and chase memories and not money. And most importantly—for me at least—is to have a close, personal relationship with my Saviour. I don't want to get to Heaven's gate and hear Him say, "I don't know you." When you have a life-threatening illness, you do think about death. This obviously leads to "What comes after death?" I believe in Heaven and hell. I believe in God and Jesus as our Saviour. And because of this faith and belief, I knew I needed a closer relationship with God. I needed my faith to deepen. And this can happen only by speaking to Him regularly and reading the Bible.

1 January 2025
Welcome 2025

I couldn't quite believe that 2024 was over and, hopefully, all cancer treatments. I had made it. Life could slowly get back to normal. Richard and I spent a very quiet New Year's evening together—it was just perfect.

For the rest of January, I revelled in the quietness, peace, and rest I had with Richard. My days were filled with sleep, reading, binge-watching Netflix series, and nipping out now and again for a lunch with Richard. Bliss!!

We even found time for a mini snowball fight!! At least, Richard called me outside and I, blissfully unaware, walked into a snowball hurled from a distance. And of course, I had to throw one back! What fun and laughter!!

29 January 2025
Time to Return to the UK and Reality

And then just like that, my time with my son came to an end. It was bittersweet. I would miss him, but I was also looking forward to getting back to some sort of “normality” or “reality.” I was scheduled to start my first caring job on 5 February. I was *so* thankful to Carol and Diana from Calm.WeCare agency. They always look out for me in so many different ways. These two women just need wings!

Before my son left the airport, he handed me a gift box and an envelope. Then he hugged me and left. My heart ached as I watched his back while he walked away. I hate goodbyes. It reminded me of something: When he was young and visited his gran, he always said he hated goodbyes when it came time to leave. Back then, I tried to cheer him by saying there can be no joyful hallos without sad goodbyes. I was reminding myself of that now.

As I opened the gift box, I saw a tree-of-life pendant. I absolutely love the tree of life. He knew this and gave me the best gift possible. The envelope held money (thank you, my love) and a note. And just like that, I was in tears. Sitting at Boston International Airport, waiting for my flight, I was crying.

I was completely overwhelmed. It wasn't just leaving Richard. I do believe that if I was not in a public place, I may have given free rein to my emotions and bawled my eyes out. Like a release valve releasing all the pent-up emotions that have been raging in my belly for months. But I didn't. I cried gently and quietly and only for a short while. And then I pulled myself together—as I always do—and continued to the check-in counter.

30 January–5 February 2025 Arriving at Heathrow

I really have amazing friends. My wonderful friend Trish fetched me at the airport. She had been my lifesaver those last few days, going way beyond help and kindness. She definitely walked the second mile for me over and over again! I am so thankful. She offered me a bed for the few days before I started my first caring assignment.

Life moves on at a rapid pace. Sometimes, nothing happens. And sometimes, loads of different things happen—some good and some not so great!

Arriving at Heathrow and hearing the British accent made me feel at home! I was glad for that.

I saw my GP the same afternoon I arrived in the UK. He made copies of reports from the doctors in South Africa and referred me back to the breast clinic where I was originally diagnosed. Then he made an appointment for blood tests. I still didn't officially know if I was in remission. However, my GP read the reports from the oncologist in South Africa and said it seemed I was in remission but that there were underlying issues that needed to be addressed. He therefore started with blood tests and referred me back to the Maidstone breast clinic.

I received the blood results, and there was an indication of anaemia (extremely low iron), liver disease, and kidney disease. A liver reading should be 5 to 35. Mine was 53. A kidney reading should be 90, which is normal. Early-stage kidney disease shows up as 60 to 89. Mine was 55. So not great, but I was scheduled to have bloods done again on 17 February. Maybe the readings would be better then. I knew that I needed to drink more water. And probably take iron tablets. And probably look at my diet. The doctor also recommended a PET scan, but the breast clinic would organise this.

I was looking forward to going back to the Maidstone breast clinic and being back in the surgeon's and oncologist's capable hands.

19 February 2025
Anger

There were moments over the past year when I was consumed by anger. Times when I thought, *This isn't fair. Why me?*

I look back at my twenties, thirties, and forties—my so-called *best years*—and feel like they were stolen from me. Wasted on a marriage that drained me. I wasn't allowed to laugh too loudly or make too much noise. Perfection was expected at all times. My days were spent protecting my children from angry outbursts and making sure they felt safe in a home that didn't always feel like one. When my husband would walk in the door, they would disappear—either to their rooms or out with friends. Anything to avoid the tension. And now I can't help but feel robbed of those years.

My fifties were different, finally filled with freedom. I won't pretend that I didn't go a little wild. After being caged for so long, I let loose. I drank. I smoked. (I even smoked "grass.") I danced. I laughed loudly and lived recklessly. I dated. I explored. I felt alive. Some of it was wonderful. Some of it wasn't—but it was mine. For the first time in decades, *my* life was *mine*.

Now in my sixties, I *should* be embracing all the things I love—travel, adventure, and new experiences. Instead, cancer had other plans. I lost a year of my life to surgeries, chemotherapy, and radiation. My days became a blur of doctors' visits, medications, needles, and endless treatments.

But it didn't end there. Now I was facing ten years of a hormone-blocking tablet that brought relentless, scorching hot flushes. It disrupted my daily life, shifted my moods, and changed how I presented myself to the world. Dressing up felt pointless when I knew my body would ignite at any moment and that I'd be desperately peeling off layers to cool down. Makeup melted off. My hair clung to my damp skin. There was nothing attractive or dignified about it.

Black was the best colour for me to wear because any other colour highlighted the fact that I was boobless. Being boobless also accentuated my tummy and made it look much larger than it really was.

And then there was the neuropathy—the constant, nagging sensation in my feet that felt like walking with wet sand in my shoes. It was not excruciating, but it was exhausting. It was always *there*.

By the time these ten years of hormone blockers were over, I'd be close to 76. How much time would I have left to truly live? Would I still have the energy and health to do the things I love? Would the cancer stay away? Would the hot flushes ever stop? Would it become easier to walk?

So yes—I got angry. *Terribly angry*. Life is *unfair*. And sometimes, I just needed to scream that into the universe. But know this: Even if I was giving in to my anger and sadness, I was not planning to stay there.

1 March 2025
A New Start

Slowly but surely, I was reclaiming my life.

My dear friends Diana and Carol, who run the care agency Calm.WeCare, placed me with a wonderful lady in West Sussex. She'd be 99 in August, yet she was still completely sharp and full of life. Sweet, kind, and an absolute pleasure to care for.

As an added bonus, she had a cat—Kushi. Oh, how I adored this cat! And dare I say, I suspected she was beginning to adore me too.

I was beyond grateful for this assignment. It was a fresh start and a chance to rebuild. My next goal was to buy a car because if there's one thing I cherish, it's my independence.

I had an appointment with my original breast surgeon on 27 March 2025. My hope? That he could help me with the uncomfortable lumps under my arms. They were not only in the way but, frankly, unsightly. More than anything, though, I was hoping to hear the words I'd been longing for: *You're in remission.*

27 March 2025 Visit to the Breast Surgeon Who Originally Diagnosed Me

I was so happy to see the doctor who diagnosed me in October 2023. I could hardly believe that 16 months had passed since then.

He was a kind, gentle man. I had to wait a rather long time in the waiting room. Sitting beside me was a lady who was clearly anxious. Eventually, she started talking to me and said she'd had a biopsy and had been called in for a face-to-face appointment with a doctor. She was afraid they were going to tell her she had cancer. Oh, I could completely understand what she was going through. I was called in to see the doctor. And when I left, she had gone. I still wonder what happened with her. We breast cancer girls are special!

The doctor told me a few things, which I will list for clarity.

1. He advised that the port stay in just in case we needed it again for chemo! I didn't know if I should panic or just quietly accept the fact that there might be a need for the port in the future.
2. He would do a reconstruction but only after at least a year.
3. I needed to lose weight. This would reduce the lumps under my arms. If there was any excess skin left at the time of the reconstruction, he would remove it.
4. He was referring me to an oncologist. Having malignant cells in a seroma is apparently extremely rare but also meant I had a very high risk of reoccurrence. He wanted the oncologist to put me on a chemo tablet or some preventative medication for a while. (It turned out that the oncologist I saw a few weeks later would prescribe a preventative drug called zoledronic acid, which would be given through the port.)
5. He wanted to change the tamoxifen to letrozole. Apparently, letrozole is the preferred hormone-blocking drug in the UK.
6. I would have a telephonic appointment with him again on 17 April.
7. He took a biopsy of the lesion on my chest.

I left there feeling I was in good hands. It gave me an inner peace. And I was thankful.

10 April 2025
Good News

I received a call from the breast clinic telling me that the biopsy taken from the skin lesion on my chest was clear. Wonderful news! At least there was no skin cancer from the radiation!

29 April 2025
Arrangements to Meet My New Oncologist

I received a call from the oncologist's rooms and would be seeing him face-to-face on 19 May. I was told again that having malignant cells in a seroma is very, very unusual. The surgeon in South Africa told me he had never come across another case like mine. The oncologist there also told me it is extremely rare to have cancer in a seroma. And that was why the oncologist and breast surgeon here in the UK were considering a chemo drug or some other drug as preventative measures.

I sincerely hoped he could help me with the hot flushes as well. Try opening a hot, hot oven and standing there for three minutes with your face in the heat. Then you will have an idea of what a hot flush feels like. All the sweat pores all over my body would explode open and release streams of perspiration.

19 May 2025 Meeting My New Oncologist in the UK

My new oncologist was at Maidstone Hospital and was an absolutely lovely man. He also had an amazing team of experts who chatted to me during my first appointment. They explained everything, and no question I asked was ignored.

He confirmed the following:

1. He wanted to put me on the preventative medication called zoledronic acid. There would be three IV treatments through the port on my chest six weeks apart. I would need to go for bloods three days before each treatment to ensure I was healthy enough to receive the treatment. Then I would have six treatments every six months. So I was facing another three and

a half years of treatment—although they were spaced fairly wide apart.

2. He was changing the hormone blocker to letrozole and decided on ten years rather than five.
3. He ordered a bone density scan and a CT scan.
4. He would see me every six months.

And as I typed this and reread it, I knew that my cancer journey was not over yet. However, I was in remission, and all the upcoming treatments were preventative only. And this made me so happy. I knew I was being cared for to the best of the medical team's ability. I was thankful for new technologies and drugs and glad that I could get them. I was thankful that this would give me the hope of having many more years of life. Better yet, I could have many more years of a reasonably healthy life so I could travel and do the things I still wanted to do and the things I love.

I was currently busy planning the flights to Naples for my Amalfi Coast walk in September. And I was planning to visit Rome when the walk ended. I knew I was being vain, but I was looking at having blepharoplasty surgery done as soon as I lost all the weight. I thought I might even have a neck lift! And why not? And after the year passed, I would possibly have breast surgery. I figured that new small, perky boobs might just "perk" me up!

I mentioned before about the BC (before cancer) and AC (after cancer). I want to share something that Princess Kate of Wales shared recently when she visited a hospital in Essex.

In her quiet yet powerful words, Princess Kate opened up about something many don't talk about:

"You put on a brave face during treatment, but the real struggle begins after."

She was speaking about her experience with chemotherapy—a journey that doesn't end when the last session does.

She said: "You put on a sort of brave face, stoicism through treatment, treatment's done - then it's like 'I can crack on, get back to normal'.

"But actually the phase afterwards is really difficult, you're not necessarily under the clinical team any longer, but you're not able to function normally at home as you perhaps once used to," said the princess.

"But it's life-changing for anyone, through first diagnosis or post treatment and things like that, it is a life-changing experience both for the patient but also for the families as well.

"And actually it sometimes goes unrecognised, you don't necessarily, particularly when it's the first time, appreciate how much impact it is going to have.

"You have to find your new normal and that takes time . . . and it's a rollercoaster it's not one smooth plane, which you expect it to be. But the reality is it's not, you go through hard times," said Catherine.

The princess was in a conversation with a group of patients, and one told her: "It can be very discombobulating, in that time when you've finished active treatment."

"Your reality has completely changed," the patient told the princess.

Catherine talked of the need for recovery time: "There is this whole phase when you finish your treatment that you, yourself, everybody, expects you, right you've finished your time, go, you're better, and that's not the case at all."

Because once the treatments stop . . . the world expects you to bounce back.

To smile.

To "go back to normal."

But the truth is, that "normal" no longer exists.

What follows is a deep emotional rollercoaster:

The medical team is no longer by your side every day.

The adrenaline of survival fades.

The exhaustion lingers.

And you're left navigating a new version of yourself—physically, emotionally, mentally. "It's a much harder process than I ever imagined," she said.

This isn't just a story of resilience. It's a reminder: Healing takes time. Not just the body—but the soul. So if you—or someone you love—is in that space after the storm, don't rush the calm.

Let it come, slowly. Gently. With grace.

And above all, don't expect to be who you were before.

You're becoming someone even stronger.

I am alive.
I am living!

Erika and me before cancer!

Sam, her husband Nic, and their son Nathan.

My son Richard, me, and Sam—all before cancer.

Last dinner with my support structure before leaving South Africa.

Mom and son. Happy times before cancer.

Time with my son in Cape Cod during the winter.

Lunchtime.

Acknowledgements

I cannot end this memoir without saying thank you, with all my heart, to several people.

Erika, my precious sister, you helped me, cared for me, carried me, encouraged me, and gave me a lovely place to rest. Thank you for the laughter, the card games, and all attempts to keep things normal.

My Sam—my most wonderful daughter—how does Mom express my thankfulness to you for all you did for me? The gentleness when showering me and helping me dress, the many trips to hospitals and doctors' surgeries. The lovely bedroom you and Nic put together for me while I stayed with you. Thank you for your healthy, delicious meals and for your endless love. Thank you for your wise advice.

Pieter, my brother-in-law, thank you for opening your home to me again. Your kindness is unmeasured.

Nic, my son-in-law, thank you for being so helpful in so many different ways. Thank you for helping Sam when she couldn't do things for me—with wound dressings. Thank you for taking care of me when I stayed with you. Thank you for the delicious barbecues. Nothing went unnoticed.

Richard, my wonderful son, thank you for giving me a safe place to recover after a year of pain and treatments. You gave me a space where I could do whatever I wanted for six weeks. I slept a lot, read, and binge-watched series that I thoroughly enjoyed. After leaving you and returning to England, I was well able to start work again—refreshed, energetic, positive, happy, and thankful beyond words.

I realised only afterwards how my illness affected my caregivers. Seeing my miserable face also caused them distress and pain. Sometimes, all they wanted was for me to just cheer up and do some activity, but my treatment often won.

I think of all caregivers. They need to know how amazing they are and what an important role they play in a patient's treatment and healing.

Lastly, I must thank Carly Catt and her editing team for their help in making this memoir readable! Thank you for your patience and for answering my endless questions with so much kindness.

If you read this memoir, I would love to hear from you about your thoughts and feelings about the book, as well as your personal journey.

Verena Masencamp has had a love for the written word since she was a young girl. She sometimes wrote poems and always devoured books. When Facebook started, she often wrote rambling, random thoughts, and many followers commented, saying she should write a book.

And then breast cancer hit. She started writing updates on Facebook, and many followers encouraged her to write a book or memoir about her cancer journey.

As much as she loves rambling, she never considered herself a writer. This is her first attempt at writing. She wanted to share her breast cancer journey and hopefully, in the process, help other women walking this road to understand it better and to know that they are not alone and there is life after breast cancer.

Printed in Dunstable, United Kingdom

66211352R00111